Testimonials

"A warm-hearted and open recounting of a lost family discovery by the author of Unlocking Family Secrets: Journey of an Adoptees' Quest for Answers. Sharon's loving and cautionary tale is an engrossing story that underscores the ways in which the new world of genetic testing has opened more doors into the human heart."

Connie Sewing, Ph.D., Family Specialist

"I read Sharon's book straight until I realized it was 2:00 a.m. and I needed to sleep. It was riveting. Though I am not adopted, it is easy to feel her need to find the truth of her birth. There were so many twists and turns to the journey to find her birth parents. She writes the difficult account of her adopted family with a historical perspective that fosters forgiveness, which I feel few could muster. It took me back to the era when I was a child and brought up feelings that I related to. I imagine this journey to find her roots and blood relatives will inspire others. It was a good read for me."

Bonnie Brown, Artist, Sonoma, CA

About the Author

 Sharon has been curious about her birth family and can now share her journey with her readers. She was diagnosed with breast cancer in 1993 and considers herself a survivor. She uses her experience to demonstrate compassion, thoughtfulness, and caring for those women (and men) whose lives have been touched by this disease. She co-founded Breast Friends, an Oregon non-profit organization in 2000, where she enjoyed working closely with patients and their families for over 20 years. One of her gifts is helping women emotionally navigate and overcome the disease; more importantly, she helps them focus on how they live their lives after their cancer, find their passion, and create their legacy.

Sharon is a born cheerleader, so in addition to her work with cancer survivors, Sharon connects and nurtures women of all ages to provide the tools of positivity, self-esteem, confidence, and inner power. Her compassionate coaching enables women to know what's important. She helps them realize what they want and allows them to create a plan to be their finest selves. In addition, she creates a safe environment for women to open up and discuss their greatest fears, dreams, and the legacy they want to create with one-on-one coaching, workshops, webinars, and retreats she facilitates.

Sharon is the author of "Thriving Beyond Cancer," her workshop in a book on Amazon. She was the assistant editor for Breast Cancer Wellness Magazine for two years. A fantastic positive magazine whose mission is to support the mental, emotional, physical, spiritual, and environmental healing needs of women facing breast cancer, no matter what age or stage of the journey.

Sharon Henifin is a Northwest girl, living in the Portland area all her life until she and her husband took to the road as full-time RVers. She is a mom, stepmom, grandmother, wife, daughter, sister, and beloved friend to countless people. Her positive outlook on life, boundless energy, and selfless spirit radiate throughout all she does, and her giving nature makes her a tremendous resource to those blessed to meet her.

In her spare time, she loves to crochet, knit, and explore any nook and cranny to find the right photograph to communicate her beautiful soul. Sharon's love for nature, flowers, and her favorite butterflies come alive in her photographs and has blossomed into a side business, God's Eye Photos and Gifts. She uses her talent as a digital graphic artist to help others create their dreams.

Sharon has earned the credentials of CN-BA, Certified Navigator-Breast Advocate, to be recognized by the medical system as a professional. In addition, she has been a Professional Certified Life Coach since 2008, using positive life coaching principles.

She believes God has a purpose for her in her work at Breast Friends, in the women's prison, and in private coaching, workshops, and retreats. Helping women of all ages overcome their challenges to become the women they were intended to be.

Prologue

DNA: Friend or Foe?

I went from being an only child to one of 12 so far. But it all changed with the handwritten letter a stranger opened that day in September. That one envelope amongst all the junk mail altered the life of a 78-year-old widow, along with many other people neither of us knew.

DNA results then revealed secret truths that were thought to be buried forever, only to open closets full of other secrets. Some of those secrets were very exciting, answering decades-old questions that could not be known without the test results. Others opened painful and scary memories or revealed truths no one suspected. So, is DNA our friend or our foe?

For me, an adoptee, it was the only way to know the truth and closure for several others in my new-found family. But for a few, it was a painful discovery of things better left unknown.

Before you spit in that cup, understand once the closet door is open, it can't be closed again.

There may be shocking secrets and information utterly different than what you've been told all your life, but it may also be the beginning of something magical. For your own protection, the uncertainty of the process requires you to understand upfront the emotional risks and rewards of discovery.

I Have Always Known the Truth

Even in the puritanical time when I grew up, I always knew I was adopted. I don't remember my parents sitting me down for this critical conversation. I'm sure they told me, but it feels like I've always known I was adopted. I remember the idea of being adopted as being positive. It was cemented in my brain because they often used the words "I was chosen" to describe my place in the family. My adopted mother and father "picked me," almost like selecting a prime cut of meat. Unlike being born to parents the customary way, where you get what you get, being chosen seemed like a better option. It appeared to normalize being adopted. They argued that having a baby naturally wasn't as special as parents selecting their child. I didn't think about it much; it was just a fact of my life. As a child, I didn't know about the absence of blood relatives or someone looking like me as I did when I was older. What did bother me was when I noticed through other people's eyes how old my adopted mom and dad were compared to other kids' parents. A friend asked me in the third grade if my mom was my grandmother. My friend's parents were much younger, most substantially younger, 15-20 years. Tom and Helen Bushby, my adopted parents, married later in life at 33 and 34 years of age. I'm sure Helen felt the pressure to marry as most young women did post World War II. Society considered a woman a spinster if she was unmarried past 23-26, so being unmarried until she was 33 was ancient. In the forties, the average marrying age was 21.5. Most of Helen's friends had been married for over a decade and had their children shortly after marriage. So, when my friends started referring to my mom as my grandmother or asking me how old my mom was, I became self-conscious about their age. It embarrassed me more each year as I became more aware of the world and the differences in my family.

Helen was the youngest of six children, only five minutes younger than her twin Evelyn. Besides being the youngest, she was born partially paralyzed on her left side. The doctor used forceps during her birth, and something went wrong. This left my mom with a lifelong disability. In 1913 birth injury litigation rarely happened. Doctors were placed on a pedestal back then, and most people didn't challenge their authority or abilities. Families accepted the results of a troubled birth without question. My mom was born just a few years before World War I. With an obvious physical impairment, Helen grew up in a cruel world when disabled children and their parents' lacked resources and were completely isolated. They were ridiculed and were taught to feel ashamed. Disabled children were called names, making their condition physical and emotional. If a physical impairment was obvious, the assumption was made that there must be a mental deficit. So along with a slight limp and a crippled left arm, people didn't expect anything of her cognitive capabilities because of her physical disabilities.

Helen grew up in her twin sister's shadow. Evelyn was instructed to allow Helen to tag along. It wasn't difficult when they were little, but it must have been terrible for both of them through middle and high school. My guess is her sister resented Helen for tagging along with all her childhood activities. As a result, Helen was the brunt of jokes and humiliation, which, in hindsight, was a huge reason she became an alcoholic later in life.

As a child, I remember looking at photographs of her, and I noticed she never seemed to smile. The photographic techniques were inferior when she was young, and it was hard to hold a smile long enough to get a good photo, but the reason was more than mere camerawork. Helen was a serious child without much to be happy about. She never felt whole or good enough through school, marriage, or most of her life. Parents, siblings, and strangers acted like she was broken and less than others, and unfortunately, she never believed anything differently about herself. She dropped out of high school and didn't finish her first year. As a teen, when many young women were thinking of dating and parties, she was stuck at home feeling sorry for herself. The Great Depression hit in 1929, and many educated adults were out of work. She didn't look for work because she had so few marketable skills plus, by the time she turned 18, it was the height of the Depression when few people had jobs. Food, gas, sugar, and other essential resources were scarce and rationed. Those years' physical and emotional impact affected the entire country, not excluding her family.

Many men defended their country during the forties when America was thrust into WWII. Like other women, Helen left her domestic duties to help with the war efforts. Like thousands of women, she emerged from the kitchen and took the open positions left by the soldiers. Now in her late twenties, Helen drove a truck during this turbulent time. She had a paying job for the first time, earning her own money and gaining a sense of independence. Reflecting on my twenties, having a job and feeling independent was life-altering. But for Helen, this was the highlight of her life. To have a purpose greater than yourself can be transformational. As a woman considered broken, to feel normal and work next to others doing the same must have been revolutionary for her. I saw one photograph of my mom from this time. She was caught jumping out of the enormous truck she was driving during wartime. She looked beautiful. She smiled from ear to ear, the kind of expression where the smile came from her eyes, making it difficult not to smile back at her photo. This photo was the only photograph I remember seeing her that happy. Not even her wedding photos captured that same smile.

Unfortunately, soon after the war ended, women like my mom, who had taken jobs to help the war effort, were replaced by men who returned home. My mom and countless others returned to their lives before the war. Back to the kitchen, back to the boredom, and back to feeling unworthy. If this had been a different time, she would have stayed in the workforce and might have been happier. Her life story would have ended much differently had she continued to work out of the home. It was a time when cooking dinner for a husband was the most crucial task of the day. She didn't have a husband or a home of her own. She lived with her parents, so she didn't fit in with all her siblings.

A few years after the war ended, she met and married Tom Bushby, a man who had been married previously and had returned from the war with all a soldier's mental and emotional scars. My dad's early life wasn't any better than my mom's. Tom's mother passed away when he was only ten years old. He was the oldest of three, so he became instantly responsible for his brother and sister while his dad worked 12-hour days to put food on the table. His dad was grieving the loss of his wife and trying to raise three children alone at a time when men didn't do much of the parenting. His father remarried immediately, and because of his abusive behavior toward his new wife and the children, this woman divorced him just as quickly, leaving the children alone again to deal with his rage. Just like my mom, he had to grow up quickly during the Depression. Tom married his first bride Grace in 1940, then enlisted in the Army and went to war in 1942. It appears from my Ancestry account that a daughter was born in 1945, one of those surprises I didn't expect to find. War leaves its kind of scars, and they divorce soon after returning from war. He met and married Helen in 1947. I'm not sure when my mom and dad's excessive drinking started, but my guess is it was soon after the wedding, if not before.

Since men and women didn't discuss their pain, feelings of inadequacy, or problems in the marriage, they found this a formula for disaster. The social activities of the time seemed to be centered around the neighborhood tavern. It was common to spend time at the local watering hole after a hard day's work to blow off steam. People didn't talk about their problems; they buried them, ignored them, and then turned to alcohol or other methods to help them cope with the pain. We do this today, but at least we can access resources if we ask for help. At least we can talk with a counselor, a friend, or a support group to help cope with difficult times. Back then, you only went to a counselor if "you were crazy" or, better yet, were sent to a sanitarium. After the war, many men returned home with accelerated rage they didn't know how to process. Women felt unfulfilled after experiencing a sense of purpose, and neither could talk about how they felt. Domestic violence was commonplace, and because women were considered the property of their husbands, women had very few options to deal with their husbands' rage. Divorce was taboo, and if one was granted a divorce, one of the parties had to be blamed. It had to be someone's fault for the dissolution of a marriage. Divorce was the worst blemish on a woman's life. Even domestic violence wasn't a good enough reason to dissolve a marriage. If a divorce was granted, a woman was labeled and shunned. She felt like a failure and was ashamed of her status. Because women like my mom were uneducated, their options were severely limited.

Many couples felt that having a baby would help marital problems. It gave women something to do other than clean the house and have dinner ready at the correct time. Unfortunately, after trying to conceive, Helen realized she couldn't get pregnant, adding to her feeling of inadequacy, unhappiness, and hopelessness.

Infertility causes friction in marriages even today. When I observed my mom's siblings, they all had trouble conceiving. But again, complex topics like infertility weren't discussed. Adoptive parents were generally required to prove a diagnosis of infertility, confirmed by a doctor, to be eligible to adopt. As a prerequisite for the adoption, a caseworker "looked at prospective mothers housekeeping" and "requested a medical report certifying their inability to have a child of their own." Women were put through a battery of medical tests to ensure that she was healthy—there is no explanation of how a finding of poor health might have affected the outcome of the adoption, so it was a bit subjective.

It seems infertility ran in my mom's family. Helen's older sister, Genevieve, only had one child, a boy; her twin sister had one girl, and the other four didn't have children when large families were the norm. Couples didn't have infertility treatments or counseling around the inability to conceive a baby. Adoption seemed like the only way for Tom and Helen to have a child, but because of my mom's handicap and my parents' age, traditional adoption agencies were out of their reach. The only way they would raise a child was to adopt but not through standard channels. Private adoption was the only method open to them in the 50s. A private adoption was a binding contract between a doctor and a birthmother who wanted to put her baby up for adoption. A lawyer got involved in making the adoption legal. Private adoption was a great alternative to the unwed mother homes, where the doctor of a pregnant girl would have a conversation about the baby's future. If the birth mom decided to put the baby up for adoption, the doctor and a lawyer found the appropriate home for the baby for a fee. The distraught pregnant girl would have her problem solved, a childless couple would have a baby, and the doctor and the lawyer would make money on the transaction.

Birds and the Bees

Most parents didn't give young people, especially women, the tools or information they needed to avoid becoming pregnant. Sex education didn't exist, and parents didn't communicate the basics about intimacy with their boys or girls. When teens found themselves in the backseat necking, whatever sex information a girl had, she got from her friends. Some thought if you were French kissing, you could get pregnant, so obviously not the most reliable information. They didn't understand how any of it worked, so many discovered the hard way and made tough decisions after the fact. If they got pregnant and carried the baby to full term, many girls would go into labor without understanding what would happen to their bodies. They couldn't fathom how their water broke or that labor pains were preparing her body to deliver her baby. How frightening that must have been. Parents rarely discussed any of it, and teachers couldn't.

Contraception wasn't available. Parents would use guilt and shame to control their daughters. Married couples on TV were only shown occasionally in their bedrooms and then only in separate twin beds. Children didn't comprehend that their parents slept in the same bed, let alone have sex. It seems preposterous now, but that's how it was.

Girls would start their periods and think they were dying. Some thought they would bleed to death. And as an afterthought, moms would say, "Oh, by the way, that happens every month." No one called it by its clinical name. Instead, Moms would say our "time of the month" or "a visit from a little friend." Even in the late 60s, I remember going to the grocery store for sanitary napkins with my mom; my dad was too embarrassed. Every woman has a menstrual cycle, but it seemed like you were the only one when you had to buy supplies. These bulky-inch-thick pads we wore for the five days of our periods seemed barbaric. We wore them between our legs, but they were attached by this elastic belt around our waists with these two gripping things that held each end of the pads. This was before adhesive that kept them in place, so they moved and leaked. Horrible, but it was better than generations before me.

When sex education started, it was taught under the guise of botany, like teaching how plants pollinate and reproduce would translate to a teenager. If intimacy was discussed, it was only between a man and his wife. I remember hearing when I was young that masturbation caused blindness in boys; of course, I didn't know what that meant then. Parents never considered that a woman might want to self-pleasure herself. Otherwise, there would have been some crazy consequences for women as well. Maybe we would go straight to hell. Abstinence was the only sex education message that was safe to talk about.

We've all heard the stories from past generations and are reminded of the taboos in these earlier times. Things have changed dramatically through the ages, yet they have stayed eerily the same in others. To have a baby out of wedlock was the worst possible shame brought on not only to the girl who got pregnant but her baby and her entire family. When that mother kept her baby, she was disgraced irretrievably, and even though it wasn't the child's fault, they were labeled "bastards." The sins of the mother are passed on to the child. Things are better today, but women have always been blamed for having sex out of the bonds of marriage.

Conversely, men were almost celebrated and left blameless when it took two to make a baby. Instead of being a bastard child, we lovingly call an illegitimate child a "love child," which creates a stigma but sounds better than the alternative. In 2009 alone, 41% of children born in the US were born to unmarried mothers, a significant increase from the 5% half a century earlier. So yes, we moved forward in some ways and not in others.

In the 1950s, when I was born, a single girl hid her pregnancy from the world, sometimes even her parents. When it was no longer possible, her parents sent her away so friends and relatives wouldn't find out. If she was lucky enough to come from a family with some means, she conveniently went to care for "Aunt Mary in Florida" for an extended period. Then she would miraculously come back thinner and incredibly sad. Hundreds of unwed homes nationwide for girls found themselves in this predicament. Places where the room and board cost was discounted to help these ladies give up their babies for adoption. If a midcentury woman dared to want to keep her baby, a full-court press was used to convince her otherwise. This included stories of how her baby would have a better life if adopted. It portrayed any other scenario as selfish if she wanted to keep the baby. Heaps of guilt and shame were used to convince the mother. Besides, she would have to repay all her expenses while living away from her parents, were practiced. These homes demanded thousands of dollars be repaid if she dared take her baby home. So even if a girl wanted to retain custody of her baby, it was almost impossible after going to an unwed mother's home. Unfortunately, she left her parent's home as a scared little girl and returned as a despondent unhappy woman. These involuntary vacations created many depressed and sullen women, not comfortable with the decisions they were forced to make.

If the woman was older or not under her parent's authority, she might tell a story about how her husband passed away in the war or had a terrible accident. She would try to live as normal a life as possible, dealing with the public shame if her secret came out. Imagine the turmoil of emotions a young woman would feel in this situation. It must have been so difficult. A young woman's body goes through many changes when pregnant. Her belly and her breasts get bigger as her baby grows and kicks. The hormones are off the chart, and the emotional changes are overwhelming with the anticipation of what's to come in the following months. Then she delivers a full-term, living, breathing baby, but it's whisked away, in most cases, without being able to hold or even see the baby. The grief and sense of loss are excruciating. Most women were instructed to forget about ever being pregnant or having a baby. The new mom was told to deny it ever happened. She was encouraged to pretend that the last nine months didn't happen and to continue the rouse and make up an elaborate story of her amazing adventure while she was away.

Babies were adopted in an era of secrecy with the understanding that their adoption records would remain sealed. Yet, in practice, many adoptees want to know their stories, backgrounds, and truths – regardless of how happy they were in their adoptive families.

It's been reported that while a million couples sought to adopt a child, only 75,000 babies needed a home. This disparity led to the rise of a black market, through which "so-called black marketeers" would charge as much as $5,000—nearly $50,000 in today's dollars—to match a child with a family.

An important consideration during the 1950s was the physical appearance of the adoptive parents. At that time, adoption practices emphasized matching in appearance, from the darkness or lightness of skin complexion to hair color, eye color, height, and weight. The rationale was that, while the child should be told they were adopted, the child's appearance shouldn't be so different from the parents' that adoptive status would be known by others just because of physical characteristics. The most popular request was for a blond, blue-eyed girl.

However, many prospective parents wanted a boy first and then a girl.

In addition to matching appearance, IQ testing was another element of adoption practice in the 1950s. Psychologists examine babies and children to match them intellectually with adoptive parents. The intent was to ensure a child would be placed with adoptive parents who could best develop above-average abilities or wouldn't be too underachieving for the adoptive parents. So, for example, parents who wanted a child to complete college wouldn't likely have a child placed with them who had tested below average. Sometimes, though not often, the birth mother was tested as well. The 1950s adoption files rarely have any medical history on birth parents and even less regarding mental illnesses or similar histories. Indeed, information on birth mothers, in general, tends to be brief, and info about birth fathers even briefer. In the 1950s, women giving their babies up for adoption were, apparently, under no constraints to identify the father. They often did, but it wasn't unusual for a birth mom to refuse to identify the father, even if she knew him. Social workers respected that decision at the time. That policy, of course, has unintended consequences for adoptees searching for their birth families. There is often no way for adult adoptees to learn who their fathers are. DNA testing alters that to some extent, but I would guess it could be a frustrating reality for many adoptees that, in the 1950s, social workers felt no pressure to include information about the father in the records.

Like most adoption history, adoptions were conducted secretively during the 19th century and before. Many adopted children were placed with other families to avoid being labeled illegitimate. In other words, the stigma against unmarried mothers and their children was enough of a social threat that birth mothers chose to place their children for adoption rather than raise them. Other reasons a birth mother placed her child for adoption could include poverty, illness, and family crisis. Like today, the choice of adoption was made in the best interest of the newborn child.

Before the 1960s, unmarried mothers were usually considered undeserving of the public benefits offered to impoverished widows and deserted wives. They were generally denied mothers' pensions, which virtually all states granted beginning in 1910, and Aid to Dependent Children, a federal program created by the Social Security Act of 1935. (Divorced women and non-white women were also excluded.)

Telling a child they are adopted doesn't sound like a big deal, but for years before my birth, many adopted parents never told their children they were adopted. They must publicly declare to the world their inadequacy to conceive a child if they adopt a child. For a woman to be unable to give her husband a child was unthinkable.

A child, whether natural or adopted, doesn't solve marital problems. Tom and Helen were no exception. After my adoption, Tom was active in my life only for the first few years. After that, he lived elsewhere most of the time and was absent for most of my childhood.

My mom never seemed happy. She watched TV, smoked Lucky Strikes, and drank beer all day. If only the emotions in that old photograph could be replicated. What replaced that smile was resentment, beer, yelling, cursing, and physical violence.

My mother's life was full of fears that caused her to be overly protective of me; I also think she was afraid to be alone. I went to school each day knowing I had to come straight home and get into my pajamas by 3:30 in the afternoon. Most days, I couldn't do after-school or evening activities. Instead, I sat on the floor in front of the TV, playing with my Barbie dolls while she sat on the couch, being sad, smoking, and drinking. My parents drank excessively; when my dad was around, they fought like cats and dogs. Verbal and physical attacks ensued. During one fight, my mom got a cigarette burn on her chest, which was the source of proof to my mother what a monster my dad was.

I remember a particularly humiliating experience when I was seven years old. My aunt and uncle celebrated their 25th wedding anniversary, and their son threw a fabulous party at home. The alcohol was flowing, and the worst possible thing happened. My mom and dad had an enormous fight right in front of everyone, and it escalated into a scene where she was carried out kicking and screaming by the police. I was mortified.

When I was 10, my childhood home was sold, and we had to move. My mom and I relocated into an apartment ourselves—a dreadful small one-bedroom apartment without my father. My mom's alcohol consumption got worse. She was drunk or asleep on the couch most of the time. Her overprotective nature worsened. Before we moved, the only extracurricular activity I was involved in was Girl Scouts. I joined a new troop after I moved, then got kicked out because my mom wouldn't let me attend the meetings. That year, my sixth grade was tough. I was embarrassed by the new school, friends, and living situation. Moving from a three-bedroom house to a one-bedroom apartment was a huge transition, but the worst part was I had to sleep with my mom. It was dreadful. Even though no one knew what was happening in my life, I felt humiliated, lonely, and isolated. Looking back on it as an adult, I'm sure money was tight. Since my mom had never worked out of the home, my dad supported us in our apartment and paid for his household.

Another explosive episode happened that year when my mom and I took a taxi to my dad's apartment. It started cordially but deteriorated quickly. The volume escalated, and the next thing I knew, a neighbor called the police. The police had to break up the fight, and my mom and I rode back to our apartment in the back of a police car. Again, as a child, I didn't understand any of the dynamics except when they were together for any length of time. They yelled at each other and threw things.

During grade school, I spend a lot of time at my cousin's place. Katie was 12 years older than me and was the daughter of my mom's twin sister Evelyn. As I grew up, I looked up to Katie. I wanted to hang around her, ride horses at her house, and spend time with her.

Even when she married Ron, they encouraged me to visit their apartment and spend weekends. I remember looking forward to any time I could spend with them. I remember their apartment. I sat on the floor and looked at all their books. I wasn't a reader then, so it boggled my mind that Katie had read all those books. My mom and dad didn't have books or magazines around, and I don't remember them ever reading to me, so it was odd to be surrounded by books in Katie's home.

I spent several weekends a year staying with Katie and Ron at their place. Then in the summer between sixth and seventh grade, Katie had a significant health issue. She had a detached retina and needed immediate surgery. Luckily, the school was out for the summer, so I could easily care for her after surgery. Ron could work while I cared for her during the day. It was a comfort to Ron to know she had someone there to care for her needs while he was at work, bringing home the money. A detached retina back in the sixties wasn't a simple surgery. The recovery was dangerous. Sandbags were placed on either side of her head so she couldn't move her head for fear the procedure would be compromised. I was there for almost two months that summer, which gave me a real sense of what it would be like to live there full-time, not knowing that was in my future. Although going home after seven weeks was tough, my cousins' home was full of activity, fun, and laughter, even during her recovery. Unlike my mom's place, which smelled like alcohol and cigarettes, the television was always on, and it was dark and depressing. While I was gone for those many weeks, my mom and dad must have patched up a little bit, or perhaps it was strictly a financial decision, but we all moved back into a house together before school started. I was too young, sheltered, or naive to understand how the bills got paid. I didn't understand how money problems and sleeping arrangements affected their relationship. The move was to a larger house, with bedrooms upstairs and down. When we moved back under the same roof, my mom and dad slept on different house floors. I'm sure it was for financial reasons, as two households would be tough on a single income. I was happy to have my dad back in the same house with me, at least for those two years.

High School and Adulting

In 1968 after graduating from the 8th grade, I spent a good portion of that summer at Katie and Ron's again. When it came time for my return, I didn't. My dad decided with Katie and Ron that I would live there full-time without my knowledge. My dad told them he worried about my well-being while with Helen. He planned to move out again and wanted to secure a better environment for me before he filed for divorce and left permanently. When I was due to go home, they let me in on their decision to make this arrangement permanent. I wouldn't follow my friends to Washington High School, I'd go to Grant High School instead, but I was thrilled not to go back to live with my mom.

The next few weeks were horrible. My mom was upset. She called and called and called. The drunker she was, the more belligerent she became. Finally, she could only yell when we answered the phone, so we hung up. We eventually left the phone off the hook since we didn't have caller ID back then. This situation understandably escalated her drinking, anger, worry, and anxiety; it all intensified. Her fear and depression spiraled downward. She was served divorce papers and knew my father was gone for good. He was still financially responsible for her since she never worked out of the home. He had to pay alimony, which didn't pay all her expenses. Shortly after the divorce papers were delivered, she was served custody papers to make my living elsewhere official. As I write this, I feel great compassion for her. All her financial, emotional, and life-changing stuff would be a lot to handle for anyone, deserving or not.

A few months passed before we had our day in court to make the custody arrangement legal. I remember I talked to the judge about what I wanted to happen. He asked me several questions, and I tried to be honest. Luckily, I didn't have to talk to anyone but the judge. My mom didn't appear in court, so she gave up her right to give her side of the story. Finally, it was official, the judge agreed to Katie and Ron being my legal guardians. My mom's harassment continued for the next several months, mostly when she was drunk out of her mind. She probably didn't remember her outbursts.

One drawback from that day in court, I was required to visit my mom every Saturday morning from nine to noon until I turned 18. I have to say, this part was dreadful, but it was a court order, so I had to do it whether I liked it or not. This court decision necessitated me to take a bus across town to my mom's depressing little apartment every week for the next four years. I wasn't thrilled about that agreement component, but it seemed like a fair trade to feel safe and secure in my new home.

My dad was happy he was no longer responsible for me. But unfortunately, since he was off the hook, that was the last time I saw or talked to him. He got me into a safe place and exited our lives permanently. I guess he divorced me too.

Even though my living situation had improved dramatically, life was complicated. Within the first several months of living with Katie and Ron, Katie had her sixth miscarriage. All her previous pregnancies had ended for some reason in the first trimester. Her doctor had given her a hormone to sustain this sixth pregnancy which seemed viable. The fetus lived through the second trimester, and it seemed like it would be full-term. Sadly, it spontaneously aborted at six months. As you can imagine, losing a baby at any point in pregnancy was devastating, but since this pregnancy was the first one past the first trimester, it was life-altering. Katie suffered a nervous breakdown. She flew to Texas for a few weeks to pull herself back together. The house was more subdued, sad, and quiet when she returned. Within a year after their ordeal, they decided not to try again. Instead, they adopted and started the procedures to make that happen. This was a few years before Roe vs. Wade, so newborn babies were more plentiful for adoption.

Katie's nursery had been set up for years but would be used for an adopted baby this time. Since they hadn't been picky about the sex of the baby, the room was kept neutral. Katie and Ron were both at work when the call came in. The baby was born. "What? The baby isn't due for another six weeks. How can that be?" I'm sure Katie was afraid that it was happening to her again. Their baby girl was born but born six weeks early; luckily, this time, the baby was healthy. After a few extra days in the hospital, Katherine Genevieve was the newest member of our household.

The story we heard from their adoption agency was that the baby's parents were married, but they had decided many years before not to have children. When her bio mom realized she was pregnant, she tried to reason with her husband to keep the baby. But ultimately, she would carry it to full-term and then put the baby up for adoption. It was such a joy to have this little bundle join the family. I was 15 when she was born, and since I lived there full-time, they had a built-in babysitter. I didn't complain; I loved spending time with Kate, my new little sister. I had been an only child up to this point, so she was a welcome addition to my life.

Katie didn't return to work at the phone company after Kate was born; instead, she babysat other people's children. She ran a tight ship, which was important when you have seven to twelve additional children running around. I remember coming home from school, and in the hallway were shoes, lots of pairs of shoes, all lined up neat and tidy. Sesame Street and Mr. Rogers were on TV when the kids got up from their nap. Sleepy children came down the stairs, ready to put those shoes back on and either head outside to play or settle in for the afternoon TV entertainment.

My high school experience was uneventful except for some everyday teenage girl drama. I was a compliant child, so I followed the rules most of the time; very happy to be where I was, and so I was a squeaky-clean kid. By the time I was a senior in high school, however, I felt pretty grown up and ready to launch into the next chapter of my life. I have worked since I was 14. I picked berries, babysat, and worked downtown for my dentist and Manning's Cafeteria. I made my own money and was anxious to move out and make my own decisions. But before I could do that, I had to get through Physics.

I was one of two girls in my physics class. I enjoyed physics but found out I lacked the math skills needed to succeed in the course. I took the algebra class I needed for physics, at the same time as the physics class, rather than the year before. The first term, I squeaked by with a C- but by the second term, my grade had fallen to a D. In my house, we didn't get D's or F's. The rule was if I got a D on my report card, I was grounded until I raised that grade on the next report card. That was nine weeks of being grounded. That seemed like unreasonable punishment, especially since it wasn't my lack of effort. I didn't know why I was struggling so much; I didn't realize about the math class until much later. Since the punishment seemed extreme, I decided to tell a little lie, so when Katie asked, "When are you getting your report card?" I would give her a puzzled look and say, "Pretty soon, I guess." Well, that worked for several weeks. One day, however, I walked into the house after work and was asked to sit down, and my boyfriend was instructed to go home now. Oooops, I was in big trouble. Sure enough, Katie had finally wised up and called the school. My report card came out four weeks before; the next one was in another five weeks. The jig was up, I had to fess up about the D on my report card, and the punishment was I was grounded for the rest of the term. The rest of the term was five weeks, not nine. I usually don't advocate for kids to lie or deceive their parents, but I felt vindicated when the punishment ended. My plan had worked.

The funny thing was that I got an F on my third term report card at the end of the five weeks and was ungrounded. I understood the principle behind grounding kids to encourage them to finish homework, study harder, etc. But that wasn't the problem. I was doing those things. I attended every class; I tried my best and studied extra hard. The problem was the math, not the effort. The story ended with my teacher appreciating my effort and passing me with a D. I look back at this experience with mixed feelings. I remembered this experience when it was my turn as a parent to dole out punishment for my kids, so several lessons were learned.

As graduation loomed over our senior class, Lynn, my best friend and I talked about moving out for months. We both had saved up money, working, babysitting, etc., so we had a cushion when we made the big move. We wanted to move into our own apartment as soon as possible. Our parents told us we could move out if we graduated first. We took them literally. June 5, 1971, was the day of our graduation ceremony. We picked out our new space, moved in our stuff, and slept in our apartment the same night as we walked across that stage for our diplomas. Our studio apartment was one large room, a kitchen, and a bathroom. We had two beds and two dressers. I had a hope chest with a few kitchen and bathroom items, and the rest came from graduation gifts to fill the cupboards and frig, so it looked like someone lived there. We shared the monthly rent of $113 per month. Back then, there were no cell phones or cable TV to worry about. We got our home phone and electricity set up and shared those expenses.

Most of this growing-up stuff seemed fine, minus a few hiccups. One hiccup happened on my 18th birthday, September 17th, three months after I moved out. When I lived with Katie & Ron, we celebrated birthdays with gusto and bravado. But this year, now that I was living on my own, this was new territory for me. My birthday approached, and nobody said a single word; it was just another day. I said nothing. I couldn't believe everyone had forgotten my roommate, boyfriend, and even my family. I was turning 18, which was a big deal, but no one seemed to notice. I didn't get a card or a call. Nobody acknowledged my big day at all. I was heartsick. It felt like nobody loved me anymore now that I was an "adult." Is that what it meant to be a grown-up? I had taken the day off from work, and after many lonely hours, I decided to make myself a birthday cake since it was clear no one else wanted to celebrate with me.

Late that afternoon, I finally got a call from my boyfriend. He said, "Let's go to a movie for your birthday." A $%&#! Movie? Really? We always go to the movies. That's what you do when you're underage. But in my passive-aggressive way, I just agreed and pouted. We left to go to the movie, and for some reason, we stopped at a restaurant near the theater to talk to his uncle. I was pouting, so I wasn't paying much attention. We walked into the restaurant and "Surprise!" My entire family stood up and yelled! Happy Birthday!! This was my first surprise birthday party. I was so embarrassed I started to cry. I had thought everyone had forgotten. But instead, I was showered with gifts, balloons, and flowers. Katie and Ron had bought me the sewing machine I had wanted desperately. The funny part was I ended up with not one, or even two, birthday cakes; I ended up with three birthday cakes that year - the one I made for myself out of pity, one from the surprise party, and my roommate came through as well. I felt like a fool for thinking my family and friends didn't love me and had forgotten my big day.

Another memorable story was when my little sister got chicken pox about a year after I moved out. I worked at the phone company by then, making $99 a week. I called Helen, my adopted mom, and asked, "Have I had chicken pox?" She said, "Yes, of course, but it was a mild case." So, I thought, I'll go over and make my baby sister feel better since I'm immune. Two weeks later, I broke out with a doozy case of chicken pox. I couldn't work for two full weeks. Missing ten days of work wasn't in the budget of a newly emancipated adult, but luckily, I had saved a little money and could keep my head above water. This was another reality of being an adult I hadn't considered. I was miserable, with gross oozy sores all over my body and no one to baby me back to health. No one wanted to take the chance of getting chicken pox; I was contagious until they scabbed over. Finally, after two weeks, they dried up enough so I could return to work, this time with scabs all over. I had never had acne on my face, so this was a real wake-up call of how it felt to have blemishes all over my face. I appreciated my clear skin a lot more after that lesson.

When I was 19, Katie and Ron added to the family again. They brought home my little brother Robert at only three days old. His mom was only 14 at the time of his birth. She was too young to raise the baby alone, and her parents weren't interested in the additional responsibility. Since I lived on my own and worked full time, I didn't connect as well with Robert until much later.

By this time, my roommate had gone off to Life Bible College in LA. I lived with a new friend who managed a Taco Time restaurant, and one of her employees was struggling. Nancy brought her employee home one night to help her out. We heard how her mom had grappled with mental illness for years and would have an episode every six months. After getting her meds adjusted, she could regain her responsibilities and her children. This was one of those unsettling times, and social services got involved. The tricky thing was that she had three younger siblings caught in this crazy-making cycle. Child Services tried to find a family to take all three little kids, but they had a terrible time making it happen. A light bulb went off, Katie and Ron were great with kids, and perhaps they would be interested in helping. I called, and they were happy to assist where they could. We then talked to the social worker and got the wheels in motion to contact Katie and Ron and quickly certified them as foster parents. They took on all three of the kids and loved being foster parents. This started an almost 20-year history of them being a foster family.

Adopted a Second Time.

When I turned 21, Katie and Ron asked me a big question. They asked me if they could adopt me. It wouldn't change anything other than when they passed away. I would be legally one of their children and potentially be heir to some of their possessions. Since I was of age, I could make this decision without telling my adopted mom about it. She didn't need to sign off or even know, for that matter. I didn't want to cause my adopted mom any more harm, so if I could make this decision alone, I agreed. I was flattered. I had been adopted twice, once at ten days old and again at 21. Not too many people can say that.

The Beginning of the End

In 1980 I found out my dad had passed away. I hadn't seen him since we went to court to finalize the custody agreement 12 years before. It was sad, but he hadn't been part of my life for most of it, so I had processed most of the feelings of loss years before he died. Unfortunately, this was the beginning of the end for Helen. Her love had turned to hate years before. This hate was the fire that kept her going, along with the alcohol she ingested daily. With one small meal a day and the calories of all the beer she drank, she barely existed. She stayed alive to hate my father, I swear. When she heard he had died, something snapped in her. She lost her will to live. She had lived to hate my father, and now he was gone. She stopped eating, drinking, and smoking. Everything stopped that day; it was like someone flipped a switch in her brain. While she could protest, she wouldn't do anything to help herself or allow us to help her. Finally, when it got so bad she couldn't fight us anymore, we could help. I found her curled up in the fetal position, ready to die. Ron came over to help me take her to the hospital. She recouped, but for the next eight years, she was in and out of all levels of care: hospitals, rehab, adult foster care, retirement homes, etc.

When my mom passed away in 1988, I remember I made a promise to myself. I vowed to make a difference in other people's lives. I remember walking out of her memorial service feeling great sadness, not so much for her death but for the life she had wasted. She lived 76 years on this earth; from my perspective, she didn't have much to show. I'm not referring to personal wealth or possessions; I'm talking about making a difference in the world and other people's lives. I'm not suggesting that everybody needs to travel the world, write a book or be a famous speaker, but I am saying that it is our responsibility to use our God-given gifts to be our best selves. My mom was an unhappy person her entire life. She wasn't grateful for what she had or what anyone did for her. Her bitterness permeated her existence and poisoned people around her. She used her emotions as weapons; unfortunately, they ultimately killed her. We all deal with difficult situations, tragedies, and challenges. How we transcend these obstacles makes us stronger and more resilient. But working through the emotions and moving past challenging events is necessary. These experiences will often be the catalyst to help us discover our strengths. Don't waste time or energy dwelling on the past or the negative aspects of life as my mom did. Like other challenges, I believe it is essential to acknowledge what you have been through and move forward.

My Early Search

I always wanted to search for my birth parents but didn't want to upset my adopted mother while she was still alive. Since Helen passed in 1988, I thought about starting that process, but by then, I had my biological child, who was four, and I was parenting my husband's two children. I loved being a mom. I couldn't imagine not being a mom. The thought of any mother giving up her child was unimaginable to me, but my circumstances were very different; I was married, had a house, and had a good job.

A friend of mine was traveling around Oregon and Washington for business, and she asked if I wanted to join her on one of her trips. She was going to Aberdeen, Washington, this time, and since I was born there and hadn't ever returned, I thought it would be fun to look around the city while she worked. Then we could spend some much-needed quality girl time together in the evening.

I was born in Aberdeen's St Joseph Hospital in 1953. Unfortunately, Grays Harbor Community Hospital had taken over the hospital building and turned it into a drug rehab center since. I remember I got out of the car and walked around, trying to comprehend the concept that I had started my life in this building in this little coastal town of Washington. Finally, I decided to go inside to have a look around. While observing my surroundings, I talked to a nurse, shared that I had been born there, and asked if she had ever heard the name Dr. O'Brien. Small world moment; he was the doctor who had also delivered her daughter. She had heard he had retired and moved to California. I found that to be an interesting coincidence. I continued my exploration of the small seaside town as I imagined how it had been so many years before.

Because adoption records are sealed at birth in Washington state, it would take a court order to open them, and only then by a third party. The adoptee has no right to have that information without the biological mother's approval. This law changed in Oregon back in 1998 but not in Washington. My coastal journey ended with more questions than answers, but it gave me more to think about. When I returned home, I got busy with life. I worked full-time and raised three children, so getting distracted from my search was easy. Unfortunately, my thoughts of my birth mother again slipped to the back burner.

The next time I felt the deep desire to find my birth mother was in 1993 after I was diagnosed with breast cancer. I had just turned 40. I didn't have the time or energy to do much other than think about her and wonder who and where she was. I had plenty of time while going through treatment and healing from surgeries but not the energy or motivation needed for anything more.

My thoughts through treatment changed to things like, "Why did I get breast cancer so young? Did my birth mom have breast cancer? Does it run in my family?" So many questions again without any answers. The answers would have to wait for another time when I was stronger physically and emotionally.

Non-ID Information

In 1996 I remembered coming home from work one day to an excited 12-year-old daughter who had just watched an informative story on Oprah. My daughter described how a woman on TV had been adopted at birth, "like you, mommy," and had looked for her birth parents for years. She had looked for answers about her birth, and so far, the answers had eluded her. Finally, she was rewarded for her search efforts when she traveled to the small town where she was born. She went to the local library and asked the reference librarian if she could look through the annuals from when her birth mother was in high school and/or graduated. After tirelessly looking through old yearbooks for several hours, she found a woman resembling herself. She felt like she saw a picture of herself looking back off the page. The resemblance was uncanny. It was like looking at herself with a 1950s hairdo and outfit.

Oprah's guest had assumed, as many adoptees do, that her mom had been serious with her boyfriend in high school; they were in love and crossed the line in a wave of passion. When she heard the news that she was pregnant and had to leave school prematurely to deliver her baby, she was ashamed and brokenhearted. It's funny how most adoptees I've had conversations with have created a story like this, the possible scenario that forced their mother to give them up. Like this woman, I had created a similar account for my birth and adoption drama.

But after her search in that quaint little town library, she had a name and a face to hold on to, and her search went from there on to the Oprah show for the whole world to hear. My daughter was so excited she wanted to get into the car that moment to drive 150 miles to the north and perform a similar search. Chelsey is and was even then a persuasive and determined young woman. So after hearing the story and with a lot of coaxing, we planned a weekend trip to drive north to look at both small libraries in the area where I was born. These were two small, somewhat depressed fishing towns on the Washington coast that could reveal some personal history. One library was in Aberdeen, and the other one was in Hoquiam.

We made the drive on a Friday afternoon but got to Aberdeen after the library was closed for the day. We decided to look around and went to the building where I was born. We talked to a couple of townspeople and told them the reason for our visit. From their reaction, it didn't seem like they had many visitors. Saturday morning, we were first in line when the library opened. We spoke with the librarian about what we were trying to accomplish, and she was eager to help us. While she gathered the old materials, we met an older gentleman who conversed with us. He was curious about what newcomers were doing in his town. He had been a resident of the area for over 30 years, but his wife had lived in Aberdeen her entire life. She knew or at least talked to everybody, knew all the gossip, and was in the next room of the library. He knew she would love to speak to us; maybe she knew my mother, stranger things happen. He seemed about the right age, so perhaps something would come of it.

Pat, the wife of the lovely man we met at the library, joined us, and we caught her up on why we were in Aberdeen. She was so cute. She told us stories, and as she spoke, I thought, wouldn't that be something if she was my bio mom or at the very least knew her? My daughter spent time thumbing through yearbooks starting in 1945. We looked page by page, particularly considering the senior portraits; the pictures were larger and easier to scrutinize. We paused as I spotted a girl who looked a lot like me. Pat said she remembered the gal from the photo. I showed Pat my 1971 yearbook photo at the same age. We stared at the image, trying to see my features on her face. There was a striking similarity. OMG, could my story be like the one on Oprah?

The girl's name in the photograph was Barbara. She had the same chin line as mine, which is distinctive, a friendly smile, a similar nose, and brown hair. Her eyes looked light; I have green eyes. We thought we had found her, but we finished looking through the final few pages in the Aberdeen library. We decided it was time to reward ourselves with a nice lunch. Even though we thought we found her, we finished the afternoon with a trip to the Hoquiam library. We left the coast with a different feeling than when we came. Pat promised to follow up with Barbara and see what she could find out.

The following week I heard from Pat as she had promised. She had made some phone calls on our behalf. Our library angel had some news. Barbara now lived in Seattle, but after Pat had chatted with her, she felt confident she wasn't my birth mom. I was disappointed but also thankful that we had gone through this exercise. This experience inspired me to do some additional research. I talked about my experience in Washington with friends after I returned. Several people gave me suggestions for my next step. One friend encouraged me to join Oregon's Oregon Adoptee Rights Association (OARA). And a similar organization in Washington,

Washington Adoption Reunion Movement (WARM) offered resources and advice for adoptees looking for their birth parents and biological family members. But, as happens to all of us, good intentions get overshadowed by life and responsibilities. I went home with full intentions of joining the Washington Adoptees Rights Movement (WARM) to help me with the search. But, unfortunately, time seemed to reduce the importance of something crucial to me a couple of weeks before, and now it's become a quiet nagging.

Several months later, I finally contacted WARM, and they suggested I contact the state of Oregon for my Non-ID Information. I had no idea what that was, but any help was appreciated. They explained that before an adoption occurs, they routinely ask some basic non-identifying questions to be filed with the adoption records. So I filled out the appropriate paperwork for the state, paid the fee, and started the waiting game for a letter to come in the mail.

A two-page letter from the State of Oregon arrived a few weeks later, all official on letterhead. I didn't understand my Non-ID information's importance until I received it in the mail. The letter completely changed the story I had in my head. The information on those two short pages said my birthmother was 23, not the 17-year-old girl unable to care for a baby. She had been married and divorced with two other children. Wow, that was totally different from my original thinking, not better or worse, simply very different. She had traveled to Aberdeen to have "the baby." What surprised me was, "She used a fictitious name on the original birth certificate." She used a different name to protect herself from her ex-husband, who would have taken away her two children if he had learned about her pregnancy. It all made perfect sense to me, especially when you think about when she gave birth in 1953.

Here's the Non-ID letter I received from the state.

Dear Sharon,

You are now registered on Oregon's Volunteer Adoption Registry for non-identifying information. The following non-identifying information is contained in the record.

The letter verifies you were born at 8:07 am on September 17, 1953, at Saint Joseph Hospital in Aberdeen, WA, to a 23-year-old divorced woman. At birth you weighed 8 pounds five oz and we're 20 inches in length. Arrangements for your placement were made through a friend of your adopted adoptive parents who learned that you would be available soon for adoption. You entered your adoptive home on September 27th, 1953. Your adoption was finalized on November 9th, 1953, in the Multnomah County Circuit Court.

Attempts were made to contact your birth mother. She was contacted by phone but refused to be interviewed in person. She stated that her attorney had told her she did not need to talk with anyone. She further stated she had placed her baby of her own free will but did not want to be interviewed. The attorney stated that in order to keep the birth of her child a secret, your birth mother assumed a fictitious name and went to the state of Washington to live with her sister until after your birth.

Your birth mother was born in 1931. She had been married and divorced in Oregon for about three years. She had either two or three children from her marriage. These children

*were in her custody. She was afraid that if her
ex-husband found out about your birth, he
would cause trouble.*

*The attorney stated that as far as he could
remember, the natural mother was tall and
slender with nice manners and apparently of a
fairly high moral caliber. He could not
remember her coloring he stated that he
believed the natural father was a salesman and
had something to do with the electrical
business. He stated that your parentage was
largely English and Scotch. Although the
mother had rheumatic fever as a child, she was
apparently cured of this, and there were no
other diseases.*

*You were described as having a great shock of
black hair, which made you resemble your
adoptive father. Your adoptive parents planned
on telling you about your adoption as soon as
they felt you would understand they planned on
raising you in the Catholic Church.*

*Although the information will not answer all
your questions this is all the non identifying*

information that can be released we hope it has been helpful to you.

Sincerely, Christie Joachim
Adoption Registry Coordinator

The reality is that when my biological mother chose to use a fictitious name to hide from her ex-husband, it also hid her from me. The chances of finding my birth mother if she used a name other than her own made a search pretty much impossible. So, with that shocking news, my search came to a screeching halt with my Non-ID letter. The blessing was I had more details about her than before, but it seemed like the end of the road. I now knew I had at least two siblings born before me. I learned how old she was when I was born, which helped me imagine her life in 1953. She raised two children on her own and then found herself pregnant. I created a new story about her to wrap my head around all this new information. Could my birth father be her ex? Even though they were divorced, perhaps they had to make up sex. Or was it a new lover, a one-night stand, or someone she was dating that would eventually become her next husband? Did the men in her life know about me? More questions, and this time I felt doubtful I'd ever know the answers. With this new information and much thought, I decided there was no reason to pursue my search since she didn't use her real name on my birth certificate. I felt like I could search for years without success, which would frustrate me more. So, after telling my family the news, I processed this information the best I could and decided to put it away forever. Perhaps I would never find my birth mother; she didn't want to be found and made sure of that by using a fictitious name on my birth certificate.

My Sister Kate's Journey

Like me, my sister Kate always knew she was adopted and was curious about her birth parents. We had several conversations about our search efforts, but in 2008 things started changing.

It all started when Kate and I rode together to Tri-Cities to show our support to our mom Katie in June. Katie's 2nd husband, Larry, was airlifted to the hospital because of his latest of six heart attacks in the last several years. Kate reminded me on our long drive together that she had found her birth mother, and she lived in Umatilla, Oregon. That opened a discussion of her recent attempts to contact her birth mother and father. Nancy, her birth mother, had responded slowly to letters she had sent but only shared a few details of her life. The last letter was returned in the mail, which seemed odd since she had lived in the same home for many years. I had offered to drive the four hours with her if she decided to return to Eastern Oregon to solve this mystery.

Less than a month later, my husband and I made a similar trip to visit close friends in the area. I shared my experience about my sister's concern when her last letter was returned with my friend. Norah has been involved in genealogy for over 30 years, so she was always interested in other people's stories. After some Internet searching, we found Kate's birth mom's home address and additional background on the woman my sister longed to meet. We hopped into Norah's bright red car and headed toward our answers down the country roads. On our way to the local Walmart for dinner fixings,

Norah & I did a drive-by to get more information for my sister. My goal was to find out if she still lived in the same place by merely looking at her mailbox. Since Norah was familiar with the area, we found the road without much trouble, and in a few short minutes, we found the house. We slowed to get a good look, and I pulled out my camera to take a quick shot of the mailbox. It had a different PO Box than the letter. We pulled up a little further, and Nancy's business sign was in place, so I again took some photos to share with my sister. The next few moments would change the course of our day.

If I had been driving, I would have continued down the street a safe distance and then turned around to get one more look and head to Walmart. Not Norah; she pulled right into the driveway to make her turn. But before we could pull away, an older lady came to the open half door of the horse arena and just looked out at us. My heart about jumped out of my chest. I was looking at my sister's birth mother. Oh, my goodness, what do we do now? Again, I would have kept going if I had been driving, but I wasn't driving. Norah started inching forward and rolled down her window. I'm sure my eyes were popping out of my head. I'm sure I looked like I had seen a ghost. I whispered in a loud, insistent tone, "What are you doing?" She said, "I can't just leave without saying something; we just don't do that in the country." I thought to myself, "Why not?" So, before I knew what was happening, she pulled much closer, stuck her head out the open window, and said, "Sorry to bother you, we are just driving around taking some pictures, enjoying the day." That part was true, but there was a lot more to the story. The woman said, "No problem, come on in." OMG, really?

My heart about stopped; Norah shut off the car and got out. She looked at me and said with a wink, "Don't forget your camera." Norah and Nancy had no problem getting a conversation going, especially after Nancy found out Norah was practically a neighbor. I just smiled and nodded a lot at this point. I tried to add to the conversation but was still in shock. Before I knew it, Nancy gave us a tour of her fantastic horse ranch, where she bred and raised Morgan horses. She was obviously immensely proud of her herd. She gave us a history lesson about the breed and why they are such wonderful animals. It was clear that horses were Kate's birth mom's life. She had invested all her time, energy, and strength into her horses and the industry her entire life. At one point, she invited us into her inner sanctum. Her office was fascinating. This is where she displayed her awards, plaques, and ribbons from floor to ceiling. I was overwhelmed by the history I saw on her wall. A lifetime of memories displayed with care. As I stared up at the wall, it was apparent Nancy's life was void of people, family, and only horses. I understood what filled her time instead of her daughter. She was immersed in her horses instead of people. A choice I'm sure she may have regretted at times, but after meeting and listening to her passion, I better understood her. I felt sad for her too. Not for how she spent the last four decades but that life as she knew it might end soon. She was already 65, and the way she walked a bit bent over reminded me of the hard work she had endured every day of her life. My assessment was she hadn't slowed down long enough to regret her choices, but there would be a time when she would.

During our tour of her impressive ranch, she allowed me to take pictures of her prize-winning horses. I took several shots making sure I widened the lens so she was also in the image. I figured I could at least give my sister a few pictures of her birth mom. She then shared her pride and joy with us. She had a two-week-old foal worth more than 25 of the other horses. She had achieved the pinnacle of success in her mind and those of her industry, yet I wondered how lonely she must be. She's lived alone all these years with no husband, children, or grandchildren.

We walked away from that meeting with photos and quite a story to share with my sister Kate. I felt guilty that I was there, hearing her stories first-hand, and my sister hadn't yet had the opportunity to meet her. I felt like a fraud. I felt like I had overstepped my boundaries with my sister. I was worried she might be upset with me. I hoped she would understand that my intention was pure, but it must have been destined. I didn't tell Nancy who I was that day. Even after I thought about it, I didn't feel it was my place to do anything besides what I did. I called my sister and shared our afternoon antics; she took it in the spirit I had hoped. She even said, "Why didn't you tell her?" I explained I didn't feel like it was appropriate. If I meet her eventually, I hope she will forgive my intrusion. I hope we can one day laugh about our initial meeting.

Kate's Birthfather

A couple weeks later, I got a call from my sister telling me her husband, Nick, couldn't be outdone by my shenanigans in Umatilla. She laughed as she explained that while Nick was on a business trip, he drove through Idaho but took a bit of a detour. So he went to Kate's birth fathers' home and knocked on his door. Without any warning, Arnold (Arney) was face to face with his birth daughter's husband. After an hour and twenty minutes, Nick left with a good feeling that Kate would soon be meeting her birth father. Arney shared stories of his life and gave his version of the adoption story. It wasn't him that wanted to give their baby up for adoption; after all, it was Nancy.

We laughed over both my adventure and Nick's. I challenged Kate on how she would move forward with both birth parents. My sister is an engineer by trade and thus needs lots of information to feel comfortable with any significant decision. She again wrote letters, and her birth father was the first to respond. After his surprise meeting with Kate's husband, he had told several people about the meeting, so when the letter appeared in his mailbox, he was excited to move forward and meet. He called Kate, and they met within a couple of weeks and spent six hours together. I'm happy to say Kate and her father had a tremendous 14-year relationship until he passed in 2022.

After all my emotions around meeting my sister's birth mother and Nick's story of meeting Kate's birth father and subsequent meeting, I decided to look for my birth mother one last time.

My Journey Opens Up Again

It was 2008, and I was a few months shy of turning 55 when thoughts of my birth mother returned with a vengeance after my sister's experience. I couldn't stop thinking about her, and the idea of having siblings I would never know really bothered me. It felt like this birthday was a turning point for some reason. I lived vicariously through my sister, who found her birth parents and wished I could do the same. After I returned home from Umatilla and met my sister's birth mother, I made a pledge to myself that I would either do everything I could do to find my birth mother or I would need to be ok with never opening that door again. It was like a line in the sand. Part of me wanted to walk away and never think about these missing parts, but I couldn't.

The official birth certificate may not be helpful, but I would go back and forth in my head and present both sides of the argument. I thought, "What if she didn't use a fictitious name? Maybe I need to see the original birth certificate myself to be sure" I knew my birth mom would be about 78, and I'd be so sad to find her gone if I didn't act soon enough. I couldn't go back in time now, but if I waited any longer, it would certainly end in disappointment. It would be a shame to find out she had died recently, and I missed meeting her. I might have had the opportunity to have a relationship with her if only I had taken this step to open my birth certificate. After some careful and thoughtful consideration, I decided I couldn't close this chapter forever without this one last effort. I didn't feel I could move on without doing everything in my power to find her. If I was going to open this can of worms, now was the time. I had the bandwidth to deal with whatever happened. I was healthy, my kids were grown and in a good place. I was in a salaried position at Breast Friends, helping other breast cancer survivors, so it seemed like the best time to pursue the search. I felt like I could handle the emotions one way or another.

I decided to spend the money to hire an intermediary to confirm the information on the non-ID letter. That investment could lead me to a positive outcome, but I would know for sure if not. I researched the best way to get my original sealed birth certificate opened. It seemed to be the one piece that would close this door altogether if the fictitious name were true or bust it wide open if it wasn't. From what I could tell from my research, I needed a person that lived in Washington to petition the court on my behalf. I found an intermediary in Vancouver, WA, to make the official request. I lived in Portland, OR, across the Columbia River from Vancouver. I spoke to Darlene on the phone, and she seemed experienced, knowledgeable, and compassionate. After that brief phone call, I decided she was the one I could trust with my money and heart for this search. After I contacted her, she sent me the appropriate forms to fill out, and the wheels were now in motion to get the answers I longed for. When I received the documents, I filled out the paperwork mandated by the State to petition the court to open the original birth certificate. I attached a check for $400 to hire Darlene to finish what I had started years before. By sending off my money and the forms, Darlene had my permission to contact the courts. Darlene sent everything needed to the appropriate department in the state of Washington. Olympia is the capital of Washington state, where all adoption birth certificates lay in dusty archives. With this action, I would know one way or another if I would ever know my mother's real name.

Darlene took me step by step through the process and explained she would receive the records within about three weeks. That meant she would have some answers by the end of August or the first week of September. She would call as soon as she got my original birth certificate in the mail. In the meantime, she wanted me to draft a letter in case we needed it. If we found her name, this letter could make the difference if my mother opened her life to me or not. Wow, that was so much pressure. I would sit down to write a letter to a woman who had given birth to me 55 years ago, wondering all the while if she ever thought of me.

I went to Seattle for the weekend to visit my stepdaughter and filled her in on all that was happening. During some downtime while I was there, I drafted the letter. I remember thinking about it, asking God to help me find the right words. When I sat down to write this potentially life-altering letter, I found that the words flowed easily out of me. Darlene had instructed me not to reveal too much information in the letter to give away my ID. This seemed weird to me, but I was as careful as possible to follow Darlene's instructions for the letter. If a letter were needed, and I prayed it would be, I wanted it to help the process so everything would move forward without a hitch.

It was a very long three weeks, but while I waited, I tried to understand how it must have been to live in the 50s. I reminded myself of my birth mother's circumstances. She was a divorced single mom responsible for two children. She then found herself pregnant during a time without tolerance or the option for abortion. Darlene also suggested I read the book:

The Girls Who Went Away: The Hidden History of Women Who Surrendered Children for Adoption in the Decades Before Roe v. Wade. It's a book written by Ann Fessler and published in 2006. It describes and recounts the experiences of women in the United States who relinquished babies for adoption between 1950 and the *Roe v. Wade* decision in 1973. It helped me understand some of the pressures women faced in previous decades without options, birth control, or abortion. I was a single mom for several years myself, and I remember the fear I felt at times. I wanted to provide a good home for my daughter, yet I didn't know what the future held for us, so it was scary. It must have been a very rough time in my mother's life, and I tried to rely on my empathy around her circumstances to make sure she understood I didn't hold a grudge or wasn't judging her for her decision.

As promised, three weeks later, I got the call from Darlene. She got the niceties out of the way and was finally ready to relay the news I was anxious to hear. In one sentence, she said, "I got your birth certificate in the mail today, and I found your birth mother." I asked her to repeat what she had just said, she did, and I confirmed I had heard what I thought I had heard. She explained that my birth mother had used a fictitious name on my birth certificate but had also signed her real name on the second line where she needed to put her signature. With that, all it took was a quick internet search, and Darlene could find her. What? How can that be? I was in shock. I had expected the birth certificate to return in the mail and hoped it would answer the question about the fictitious name. I hadn't even fantasized this could happen or happen so quickly. I had hoped Darlene might be a super detective and would eventually find her, but I was stunned by the news. She went on to say that her telephone number was non-published, but she did find an address so we could try to communicate with her by mail. Darlene couldn't give me any specifics until my birth mom agreed to the contact. She told me she lived in Oregon and had already found my half-brother, who also lived in my state. She would continue to look for my other half-sibling, not knowing if it was a sister or a brother.

OMG, she found my mother, and she found my brother. Would I ever be able to meet them? Would I be able to know their names? It was all on the shoulders of a woman who used a fictitious name so she wouldn't be found. The big question remained; would she open the door to me? I would have to leave this one to God, too. If it was meant to be, it would happen. At that point, I hung up the phone and realized that my letter would indeed be mailed. Darlene would send the letter with the forms needed to give me her contact information. I re-read what I had written to ensure it didn't come across as judgmental or pushy. I merely told her how I felt about being able to get to know her. After re-reading the document, I said a little prayer, tweaked a few things, and sent it to Darlene. Overall if this was the only thing my mother heard from me, it said what I needed it to say. I said another little prayer to open her heart, and if it was His will, I would be allowed to meet this woman. I remember retrieving a couple baby pictures from their album, and how I kissed them carefully. I put them in an envelope with the letter and sent them to Darlene, hoping that the next time we talked, it would be to get my mom's contact information.

The Letter

Dear Birthmother,

I hope this search will find you safe and willing to open your life to me. I wanted to reach out to you now before it is too late. I have searched for you a couple of times in the past. After getting my non-ID info back in 1996, I was surprised and discouraged. It surprised me because the information described a woman differently than I had expected. I had fantasized about a girl getting pregnant at 17, still in high school, and unable to care for a baby. After reading the actual story, my heart went out to a woman who was trying to protect her children from what her ex might do if he found out about what society would consider a mistake. I was disappointed because the words led me to believe I couldn't find your real name, thus making a search impossible.

On my next birthday, September 17th, I will turn 55. I felt I needed to either do this last search or give up the idea for good. I hired an intermediary to get my original birth certificate, and adoption decree opened. The intermediary, Darlene, asked if I wanted to write a letter. I honestly hadn't considered writing, but if you are reading this, I feel it's worth one last effort to reach out to you and hopefully have the opportunity to talk before one of us leaves this earth.

A little bit about me, I am married; I have three kids, a biological daughter and two stepkids, one boy and one girl. My husband has a son and daughter and two stepkids. We have a couple of grandkids and enjoy spending time with them, even though some live out of town.

I was diagnosed with breast cancer 15 years ago, shortly after turning 40. I underwent six surgeries, including a double mastectomy and six months of chemo. Because I was diagnosed so young, I wonder if you have gone through breast cancer and if I have the gene mutation. Unfortunately, my daughter has breast cancer on both sides, so I would really like to know if you or my biological father has breast cancer in the family. This is probably the most important question I have for you.

I worked for a large corporation for over 30 years in sales, sales management, and training before retiring in 2006. Now I am honored to work for a nonprofit organization I helped to co-found where I help women and their families go through the breast cancer journey. I believe this is the purpose I was born to do, and I feel fortunate to be able to support others through their traumatic experience.

My adoptive parents loved me and tried to give me a good life, but unfortunately had their own troubles. However, I believe they did their best under their circumstances. I was adopted a second time after I turned 21 by family. This is a long story that I would love to have the opportunity to share with you someday soon.

*I would like the opportunity to meet you, talk to
you, find out more about your life, and share
my life story thus far with you. I am a nice,
easy-going person with a positive attitude, and
I am fairly certain that some of that comes from
my biological parents.*

*I would like to have the opportunity to find out
about and meet my half-siblings and perhaps
have a relationship with them in the future if
they are interested. In addition, I would like to
know the name of my biological father, so I
might also talk to or meet him as well if he is
still alive.*

*I understand some of the difficulties you must
have gone through as a young woman,
divorced, with children finding yourself
pregnant back when our world was very
judgmental. I understand the need to hide your
pregnancy, use a fictitious name, go to a distant
city, and give away a child under these
circumstances. Please allow me to get to know
you and tell you in person that I don't blame
you for giving up a child for adoption or hiding
your identity. In fact, I think it took a lot of guts
to be a single mom in the 50s. I also went*

*through a divorce and found myself a single
mom, so we have a lot in common. I have had
the ease of birth control and a much-relaxed
view from the society around divorce you didn't
have the fortune to experience.*

Thanks for giving birth to me, Sharon.

Here is the baptismal photos I sent.

I tried to measure my expectations regarding this emotional time. I didn't want to set myself up for massive disappointment. I didn't want too much emotional investment or to create a story in my head that was larger than life. You know, the one where she has been looking for me for all these years, and her life wouldn't be complete without finding me. We all would love that to be the case, but reality can be harsh. What if I do find her and when she meets me, then rejects me? What if she never wants to meet at all, like Kate's bio mom? I told myself the worst-case scenario to keep my expectations in check, but I bounced from one extreme to the other. I hoped my reality would be somewhere in the middle.

Darlene described how the next phase would go. My birth mother would get the letter, and if she wanted to have contact, she would call Darlene. It could be as quick as a few days, or she may never hear from her. So, the waiting game started again, with my bio mom holding all the cards. If she didn't want to be found, all she had to do was ignore the letter. If she didn't respond to the letter, my hands were tied. My 55th birthday was in a week, and I fantasized she would make contact on my birthday. Unfortunately, my birthday came and went, and I heard nothing. I tried to remain positive, but it was a challenge.

The next few days were some of the busiest of my year. The long weekend was filled with breast cancer activities culminating Sunday with the Race for the Cure. I came home that Sunday afternoon, very tired, ready for a quick nap since I had been up since 4:30 am. When I got up from my nap later that day, I noticed I missed a call from Darlene. This could be the call either opening the door or sealing it forever. Without checking the message, I called the number, and unfortunately, the call went straight to her voicemail. I then checked the message, and it didn't reveal my birth mother's intention, so I went back to the waiting game. Luckily, it wasn't long before I got the call back from the intermediary. She sounded happy. I listened to her tone before the words penetrated my awareness. "She wants to meet you," was all Darlene said. "Really?" She had called on one of the most important days of my year. It wasn't my birthday, but it was significant all the same.

Only four days after my 55th birthday and the afternoon of the biggest breast cancer event of the year, I asked, "What happens next?" Darlene explained that she needed to mail my birth mother some additional paperwork. She'd need to sign and return those forms, and this would legally allow Darlene to give me my birth mom's contact information. She could give me my original birth certificate once the paper was signed and returned. The document symbolized the beginning of my life, and I would soon have it in my hands. But, of course, she could change her mind and not sign the form, again closing the door for good. Darlene told me it could take up to two weeks to get the paperwork returned. So again, more waiting.

I worked hard to put this whole process in the hands of God, but at times I would pull it back and obsess about it. Then I'd recommit to letting it go, knowing God knew what was in my best interest. It felt like it was moving forward, but this was my opportunity to trust God to figure out how it would work out.

Six days later, I received the call from Darlene. I was having dinner with my husband, his daughter, and son in law. Throughout dinner, my phone beeped, reminding me I had missed a call. Before I looked, I waited until dinner was finished and the dishes were in the dishwasher. I checked my phone to see who had called. My stomach did a flip when I saw Darlene's number. Again, I didn't check the message; I simply pushed the button to call her back directly. The thoughts in my head collided. The phone rang and rang, I was afraid it was going to voicemail, but then she answered. All I said was, "This is Sharon." Without another moment of hesitation, she said, "Your birth mother has decided to allow you to contact her." My heart just about jumped out of my body. I was elated. Darlene said, "She knows your name is Sharon. Her name is Diane. With that revelation, I felt perplexed. I paused and said, "Diane Lewis?" She said, "Well, yes. That's the fictitious name she used on your birth certificate. There were two places to sign; one said Diane Lewis, and the other showed her real name." "Her real name is Diane Justine Knievel. Hannaford is her maiden name, and Knievel is her married name." I hardly heard her; I was still stuck on Diane Lewis. How did I know that? Diane is the name I remembered as a child; I remember fantasizing about Diane Lewis being my birth mother. I don't know if I was told her name was Diane when I was a child or if I'd overheard it, or what? All I knew was that name had been in my head since I could remember. She said, "If you're sitting down, I can give you her contact information." I got some paper to write on and took down her information. "She lives in Bend, OR," and then gave me her telephone number. I now knew my birth mother's name, address, and telephone number. She told me, "She has a daughter living in California and a son in Portland. She's looking forward to your call." That meant the ball was in my court, she opened the door, and now all I must do was walk through it. I knew my life would never be the same after I made this phone call. This would change my life and the lives of my birth mother, her two adult children, my children, and other family members. The magnitude of this information was overwhelming.

I thanked Darlene for her help through this process. She sounded thrilled that she was able to help. She confided in me then that most women from this generation DO NOT open this door. Because they had been told so many times to pretend the birth never happened and to move on with their lives, many women can't open their painful past. Even though I paid Darlene for her services, I wanted to meet her and thank her in person. I wanted to hug her and tell her what this meant to me. I told her I would be sailing on the Columbia River the next day and wondered if we could meet. She told me her son was in the hospital in Oregon, and perhaps it would work. I told her I would call her when I was at the river, and we could find a place to meet. I was so excited to get off the phone and call my bio mom. I couldn't wait until I got home that evening to make the call, so after I told everyone the news, I regained my composure, went to a quiet part of the house, and dialed the phone number. Even though the official search was just about two months, it had been 55 years in the making. I gathered my thoughts and made sure I had a paper and pen to take some notes. So many thoughts were swirling around in my head, so many emotions all colliding in my brain at the very same time.

I hadn't planned what I would say; I just knew I needed to make this call before I lost my nerve.

After a few deep breaths, I dialed her number. "Diane? This is Sharon." I remember those few words, but the rest is rather a blur. I asked her a few questions but didn't want her to feel like I was interrogating her. She answered all my questions and reiterated several things she had already told Darlene in her previous conversation. One of the questions was about my birth father. She explained that she didn't know for sure who my father was. She was in a bad place back then, divorced with two young children. She was living with her mom and was having a hard time. She explained how she got drunk on New Year's Eve and was picked up by the police. She only remembered getting pregnant and thought it was the police officer, but she never knew his name or anything more. Because of being intoxicated, she had no recollection of the night. From her description, it appeared I would never know who my father was. Under these circumstances, I'm sure he had no idea I existed and thus wouldn't ever look for me.

By the end of our 45-minute conversation, I had expressed my desire to visit Central Oregon to meet her. My schedule was flexible, so I could take a few days when needed. I thought visiting her in person would be the best way to learn as much as possible about her. Phone calls were great, but since she was only three hours away, I wanted, no needed, to see her expressions, her body language, and mannerisms.

She agreed and said she would like to meet face-to-face. She said her only problem was she had a bunch of boxes that needed to be moved. She said she moved into this apartment about a year ago and hadn't finished unpacking. I said she didn't need to worry about that; I would stay elsewhere. She insisted I stayed with her and wanted me to call in a couple of days to make sure she could get it all cleaned up. I explained I would help her, but she didn't want me to work when I visited. Finally, I agreed to call her again, and we could firm up the plans. I hung up, feeling rather numb. I had just talked to the woman who brought me into this world at St Joseph's Hospital in Aberdeen, Washington, on September 17th, 1953. Wow, it was unbelievable. The more I thought about it, the more I was overwhelmed with how a simple phone call could change everything. Besides being a mom, I have an older brother and sister related by blood. I had so many thoughts flooding my brain; I couldn't decipher my feelings. I remember coming back down the stairs with a dazed expression on my face. "Well," everyone said. I told my family what we discussed and how good the overall conversation felt. I kept remembering bits and pieces and talked about it most of the way home that night.

The next day was busy; I spent the morning at the women's prison volunteering with the Breast Friends cancer support group. This is where eight to ten women joined us every other Sunday morning to talk about cancer and how to manage their emotions. Women in prison have literally no support when diagnosed with cancer. Being diagnosed is terrible enough, but while incarcerated without access to accurate information, emotional support, or family and friends, cancer can feel like a death sentence even if caught early. My mind wandered that morning while in the prison support group. I mentioned my situation and ended up sharing a part of the news. I couldn't talk about it enough. Talking about it helped me process my emotions, so I was thankful for others to be good listeners.

On the way from the prison to the sailing event, I called Darlene to see if we could meet. I had picked up a card and a pretty bouquet of flowers to show my appreciation and hoped I would give them to her in person. We connected, and sure enough, she would stop by the yacht club to meet a little later. I stood impatiently in front of the club for over 20 minutes, and finally, she appeared with her husband. I was able to thank her in person, give her a small token of my gratitude for her efforts, and tell her about the phone call my birth mom and I had shared. I also shared I'd be going to Bend later in the week to meet her face-to-face. She was delighted for me. That afternoon, a friend & I were invited to participate in Sail for the Cure, a great fundraiser for Susan G Komen for the Cure. We were both invited to sail on a fabulous sailboat on the Columbia River. It was a beautiful day with a breeze, a perfect day for sailing. After a magnificent day on the river, my phone rang. I hesitated to answer it since it wasn't a familiar number, but for some reason, I grabbed it.

"This is Sharon," I said. "This is Mike, your brother; I understand you're my sister." Oh, wow, you're calling me. After the shock of hearing this man's voice on the other end of the line, I walked to a quieter place, and we talked for quite a while. Finally, he said, "I hear we live close; you live in Tigard, right? Yeah, I live in SW Portland. I probably live three miles from you." Mike, my newfound brother, explained that he was in Bend visiting our mom when she got the letter. She told him about the letter. She asked Mike what she should do. They talked about it for a bit, but bottom line, Mike's reaction was, "Of course, you want to contact her, and if you don't, I will." So, I have Mike to thank for giving her the little push and the encouragement to open that terrifying door. When you dissect this, she didn't need to mention it to him either, so I must give her credit for her willingness to discuss it with him. Since no other living person knew about me, to bring this topic up must have been scary for her, but she did it. She had to admit to her son that she had a baby in 1953 when he was only two and a half and felt she had to put me up for adoption. Boy, I wish I had been a fly on the wall for that conversation. He didn't have a great relationship with Diane. Mike and she had only reconnected a few years earlier after over a 30-year separation. He was raised by his dad and his new wife, who didn't appreciate having him around. He felt abandoned by his mom, who had given him up to his dad when she found herself pregnant with me. He felt like she didn't want him, and he didn't feel wanted by his dad either.

Until now, he hadn't understood why she abandoned him, but now the pieces were starting to fall into place. He didn't know she had tried to get him back several times until he and I looked at court records together a couple years later. He explained to me how he didn't remember her from when he was little and only saw her once when he was 22. He was already married and had a child of his own.

Unfortunately, that meeting ended poorly. He was in his late 50s when he attempted to rebuild a relationship with his mom again, who felt like a stranger. Since I was on the river that day, having such a personal conversation wasn't easy. The noise and lack of privacy made it tough to talk. But before we hung up, he said,

"I hear you want to go to Central Oregon to visit Mom. I explained my intentions, and before I knew it, he suggested we drive over together. He was retired, so his schedule was open. He also wanted to meet me and participate in that initial meeting. I agreed it would be great to meet him and spend time together. He offered to get his timeshare in Bend for the night, and I could get to know my birth mom in a comfortable neutral place. I felt good about the offer, so I agreed. He would pick me up at home and drive to Bend together.

After I hung up and the exhilaration subsided, I played back the conversation and what I had agreed to and realized I didn't know this man. He could be crazy, a murderer who knew what could happen to me if I just got in his car blindly. I decided this wasn't a safe decision without at least meeting him first and getting a sense of who he was, so first thing Monday, I called him back and suggested we meet for coffee on Tuesday. This way, we could get to know each other a little bit better, and I would feel safer getting into his car and driving three hours to Bend. Since he lived only a few short miles away from me, finding a place to meet was simple.

After we hung up, I was in shock again. Everything was moving so fast. I was anxious but excited to meet Mike. He told me he planned on riding his motorcycle since the weather was beautiful and he would be easy to spot. I pulled into the Starbucks at the precise time we had agreed on, and there he was, sitting at an outside table with his gray beard and a do-rag on his head. I parked my car and walked right up to him with a big smile on my face. We hugged as soon as we met, then I grabbed a coffee and joined him. We didn't stop talking for two hours straight. We could have talked for several more, but I had another appointment, so we had to conclude our meeting at the two-hour mark. I hated to leave, but I didn't want to run out of things to talk about on our long drive either. Anything I had to say could wait for a couple more days. We both understood intuitively we wouldn't have any trouble filling the time as we drove the three hours to Bend on Thursday. I had my personal safety questions answered and knew in my heart; he was a good guy. I was thrilled to feel so connected to someone that was a blood relative.

I kept my expectations to a minimum on how our meeting would go, but Mike was extremely easy to talk with; he did most of the talking. Some of the conversation was about his growing up and how crappy it was for him. Even though this was my story, I felt Mike wanted to make sure I heard his side of the story before I heard Diane's. Spending more time with Mike gave me the impression I was in for a dose of a dysfunctional family. I wasn't wrong, but I loved him anyway from our first meeting.

I knew I needed to lay down my boundaries, so this visit wouldn't be a platform for Mike to show me what a lousy mom Diane had been to him. I learned a long time ago there are two sides to every story, and the truth was somewhere in the middle. Thursday couldn't come fast enough. Since our meeting at Starbucks ended quicker than expected, I knew it would be a lively drive. Mike drove to my home; I invited him for a minute to share some of myself and meet my husband before we left.

I hopped into his car like we were best friends, and we didn't stop talking until we got across the mountain to Bend. Mike had a great dry sense of humor, so he kept me laughing when we weren't debating topics. As we entered Bend, Mike got a phone call. After he hung up, he said, "Oh, by the way, that was from Vicki, our sister. She's driving up from Northern California to meet us as well." My initial reaction was, "I'm going to meet my big sister for the very first time on the side of the highway? Okay, nothing else has been normal about my life, so why not?" We weren't very far away from my birth moms' home when he pulled over to the side of the road. Within 10 minutes of pulling off the highway, there in the rearview mirror, another car pulled up behind us.

Vicki had made excellent time driving up 97 from Redding, CA, to Bend, Oregon. This was Mike's full sister, my half-sister. We jumped out of the car and did a quick introduction, "Hi, I'm Sharon, your sister." "Hi, I'm Vicki; I guess you're my sister." We hugged enthusiastically, jumped back in our cars, and finished our drive into Bend. Seemed like a rather odd meeting, but we would have more time that afternoon and evening to get to know each other. Hopefully, we would have years, but I couldn't think that far ahead. I wanted to savor the day, and if we had a future, I would appreciate it then.

Vicki was born in 1952, about 18 months after Mike was born and 11 months before me. She had lived in California with her husband for many years and visited her mom in Bend maybe once every year or two. She was going with us to the timeshare. Mike rented a lovely three-bedroom place at Eagles Crest Lodge near Bend for the three of us to stay the night and further get to know each other. I was okay with the arrangement as long as I had some alone time with Diane.

We pulled up and parked in front of Diane's apartment. I looked up before I got out of Mike's truck and saw a white-haired lady on the third-story balcony. I asked Mike if that was her, and it was. I got out of the car and waved. She waved back and hurried to the front door to let us in. Diane hadn't seen Vicki in a long time, so this was an excellent day for Diane.

She would see her son Mike, who had been close to her for the last few years since her health had been challenged, her daughter Vicki from California, and me, the child she thought she would never see.

We walked to the door, and as we reached it, she was a lovely older woman with white hair and a friendly smile. I said hello and gave her a small hug; the others did the same. We all walked into the lobby, and there was one of her neighbors. With a big smile, she introduced all of us as her children. She said, "This is my daughter Sharon, my daughter Vicki and my son Mike." Holy Cow, one minute I didn't know her at all, and then the next I'm being introduced as her daughter. That felt incredible. We made our way to her apartment, and I noticed how well she was getting around. After I talked to her a few days before, I thought she sounded frail. However, she was getting around okay, not using a cane or a walker, and didn't seem to have any obvious health issues. I was pleasantly surprised since she was already 78. Part of me thought about getting older, and I used her to gauge my future. Later I found she used oxygen several times a day, but otherwise, she seemed to be doing well.

We went to her apartment and got some of the niceties out of the way. I finally took the floor for a minute. I said, "First, I want to thank you for opening up your life to me after all these years." I was overwhelmed with emotion for the first time since this started. I got choked up, and after I regained my composure, I finished by saying I looked forward to getting to know everyone better.

Diane explained that she had divorced her first husband, Hank, after having two children, Mike and Vicki. Back in the 50s, it was common for the mother to get custody of the children in a divorce situation. But when she found out she was pregnant, it frightened her to think her ex-husband might try to take her children away. So, she hid her pregnancy from her ex-husband and the rest of the world. The only people that knew about Diane's unwanted pregnancy were her mother, who she lived with in between marriages, and her brother and his wife. When thinking about being a single mom and what I went through in 1996, I remember how scary it was. I had the benefit of being educated and a good-paying job. Diane wasn't educated and had no career, so making ends meet was always stressful. In 1953, most women didn't think they could survive without a husband, especially with children. Diane used what God had given her: her good looks and sexuality. She did what she had to do to survive.

Diane's older brother Richard and his wife lived in Aberdeen, Washington, where I was born. She escaped her life in Portland when she couldn't hide her pregnancy any longer. So, at around six months along, she went to Aberdeen to finish her pregnancy and give birth in secret. She tried to be proactive and asked her ex to take Mike for a while since she needed to go out of town. He was the type of man who was entirely caught up on the male child, first born, and being his heir and all, and she knew he would notice if she left town with Mike, so she figured this was the best way around it. She was sure he would make trouble for her if she mysteriously left town without leaving her son with her ex. He didn't ask questions, so off to Aberdeen to her brothers, she went with daughter Vicki in tow to deal with the shame and uncertainty of her future. She had intended to get her son back after she was settled again. Unfortunately, that proved more difficult than she imagined. She went to court three separate times without success.

I had hoped for this reunion day my entire life, and it was going so quickly. So far, it had gone well, not too many weird pauses or empty moments. We decided to grab a bite to eat since we were all starving. We picked up Dolores, my aunt, Diane's younger sister, to join us for lunch. We all had a lovely lunch, and Mike generously paid the bill. I offered several pieces of information about my kids and how my youngest, my biological daughter, wanted to meet everyone. We left the restaurant to figure out the next steps, Mike wanted to get checked into the chalet, so after a bit of discussion, I suggested Diane, Dolores, and I go to my aunt's home and that I would get some time to talk to Diane. Vicki and Mike would check in at the resort, and we would all join them shortly. The three of us went to the house and reviewed the paperwork I had brought.

Dolores seemed much warmer than Diane, but I chalked it up to nerves. But after getting to know them both throughout the years, I think my original assessment was correct. Dolores offered us food and drinks while we looked through more photos and listened to stories. She was more of a hugger and seemed to share her life easier than Diane. One unexpected aspect of this meeting was I learned that Dolores was interested in tracking her ancestors. We talked about a few grandparents I hadn't heard about yet. I took notes to capture all the details as fast and furious as possible. Finally, the reality hit me; these were my ancestors too. Wow, what a concept.

I read them my Non-ID letter and original birth certificate and explained my search's different elements. I asked some very specific questions. I'm sure Diane felt a bit on the hot seat, but it couldn't be helped. I had a big question about the fictitious name on my birth certificate. Besides my birth father's identity, it was the most confusing part of my story. She looked at me bewildered and said she didn't remember using a fictitious name. We looked at the birth certificate and agreed that there was a different name, but she did not remember signing two different names. When I asked her, she said she didn't know anyone with the last name of Lewis. She repeated that she didn't know the birth father's name, so that wasn't it. But where had it come from? She was 78, and when she was 23 years old, she gave up a baby after repeatedly being told to forget this ever happened. I guess she did. I asked many questions from all different directions and got the same answers. So that mystery is still in place. Later I asked my adopted cousins, Fred and Katie, and neither remembers anything about the name Diane Lewis. I still wonder where I heard it.

Diane explained how I was conceived in more detail. She told me she lived with her mom after divorcing Mike and Vicki's dad. They got along great most of the time. Her mom graciously helped babysit Vicki while she worked. It was a huge help, but her mom wasn't happy when she wanted to go out to a party or have a break for an evening. She decided to go out for New Year's Eve, and she and her mom fought about her plans. She left anyway, upset. She got drunk and drove home intoxicated in the middle of the night. She was pulled over by a motorcycle police officer. She said, "Instead of getting an expensive DUI ticket, I got you." OMG, are you serious? This police officer traded sex for a ticket.

So, when you put this story into the context of the midcentury, women did not have personal power, and what power they had seemed to encircle their sexuality and used it to manipulate men. Today it is hard to imagine a traffic stop turning into a sexual encounter, but that is what happened to my birth mom. It blows me away that this could happen, and my guess is it happened more often than I would like to suspect. Today, sexual harassment is being exposed publicly, and the aggressor is being shamed rather than the victim of the abuse with the #metoo and #timesup movements. This behavior has existed for centuries, so understanding the context allows us to better understand the times. It was the 50s, but wow, that was a lot to wrap my head around. Perhaps it happened a lot, but it was hard for me to fathom that it happened to my birth mother. The word rape was thrown out there, but Diane then sucked it back in. I'm not sure she believed it wasn't consensual. She confessed she didn't remember much of the night's activities because she had too much to drink. It sounded like the police officer had undoubtedly taken advantage of this drunk girl, but it probably wasn't rape. Unfortunately, as the story unfolded, it didn't sound like I would ever find my birth father. Diane didn't know his name or anything other than he was a Portland police officer.

She told me she married Fred, the navy man, six months after my birth. She said she met him the following New Year's Eve and married him three months later. She said she felt fortunate to find a man willing to take on her children. When they were settled down, that's when she tried to get Mike back several times, unsuccessfully. We talked candidly about the time and the difficulty of the situation. Dolores didn't know about any of this until I first contacted Diane. That's when she divulged the details to her sister about the months she stayed with their brother Richard and his wife, Betty. This was a lot for all three of us, but we kept it together.

Then the conversation moved to my adopted parents in more depth. She asked me how I felt my parents were as parents. I remember saying, "I know they did the best they could, but honestly, they weren't great parents." They both had many problems going into their marriage, and adopting a baby wouldn't fix any of those issues. In fact, a baby made it way more complicated. When the drinking escalated from social to an addiction for them both, that colored my life. Diane was quiet for a while and finally said she was sorry; she had hoped for a better life for me. I mentioned the adoption between a doctor and a lawyer, and I could see her facial expression change. She revealed that her doctor said he was interested in keeping me for himself. It sounds like his interests; his intentions were strictly for financial gain. $500 in the '50s was like $5000 now. It wasn't a drop in the bucket post-war. It was 20% of the average cost of a home in 1953. They split the $500, but the physician made my mom believe he was adopting me for his family. Diane was extremely disturbed by that. She thought I was raised by her doctor and his family all these years. This shouldn't surprise me when you consider this was in 1953.

Women didn't have the respect of most men back then. But when she was told that a man she respected, her doctor, would adopt her child, that would be the happy ending she had hoped for.

Mike and Vicki called to say they were all checked in to the resort, and we could join them in the chalet anytime. The three of us left to pick up Dolores's daughter, who lived on the way. Debi is a little younger than me; she was a great addition to the mix. We reached Eagle Crest, and the four of us walked in together, all a little anxious to know how the next few hours would unfold. Stories and old photos started to fly when we were all at the chalet. I brought some pictures throughout the last 55 years to show a smattering of my life thus far. I had pictures of my husband and children and some information about Breast Friends, the organization I had started with a friend in 2000. I had an old photo of when I was a disco dance instructor in the late '70s and early '80s. I hauled out the pictures of myself as a child, then lots of photos in my twenties, short hair, long hair, dressed up or down, even some when I was a clown. I tried to give them a glimpse of what made me who I was. I came prepared, so if we ran out of conversation topics, these photos would help remind me of times in the past when I was nervous.

It was great to be part of this evening. Mike hadn't known Debi well either, and Vicki had been in California for a long time, so she didn't see her mom, aunt, or cousin often. It was a family reunion, and I was happy to be a part of it. Of course, I didn't share their memories, so I kept quiet most of the time, just trying to digest everything. I shared my own stories during the same time frame since we were all so close in age. I heard about other family members that couldn't attend and hoped to have the opportunity to meet them in the future. It was great to see all the photos, hear the stories, and just be able to observe everyone. We took a flurry of photographs, many of which turned out great. At one point, I think we had four cameras' going, so if you were snapping the photo, it was a juggling act to get them all done before the rest of the group got restless and changed positions.

Photos of our First Meeting

Sharon & Diane 2008

Mike & Vicki 2008

Dolores and Debi 2008

My New Family

Oh, By the Way, Again

We spent the next few hours in conversation and laughter. Then, when I was finished playing show and tell with my life, it was Diane's turn. That's when it happened, "Oh, by the way, you have two more sisters." What, more siblings?

Diane had married Fred, a Navy sailor from Portland, six months after I was born; she married in Stevenson, WA., where she'd also married her first husband. Young couples traveled in droves to Stevenson because they could get their marriage license AND get married on the same day. This wasn't the case in most places; downtown Portland, just 46 miles away, had a three-day waiting period to marry.

Fred was gone to sea more than he was home. He would be gone for months, home briefly, and off to do another mission or assignment. Diane shared photos of her three girls when they were young, most without Fred. I'm sure Mike felt as weird as I did during this part. He should have been in those photos with the girls.

He was almost as much of a stranger as I was since he didn't grow up with his sisters either.

Diane and Her Son Mike in 1951

Cari is my next sibling, born a couple of years after me. She also lived in Redding, CA, so Vicki saw her occasionally, but I got the impression they weren't that close emotionally, just in proximity. Unfortunately, Diane didn't have a relationship with her, and I sensed there was a lot more to this story. Finally, Loni is the baby, born a few years after Cari. She was the real mystery, as no one had seen or spoken to her in over 20 years. They thought she lived somewhere in New Mexico or Arizona.

After listening to some of these stories, I thought my dysfunctional family may have been a blessing in ways I had never imagined. At least I never doubted that my mom loved me. She drank and made some bad decisions, but I knew she cared as best she could. Unfortunately, I got the impression that wasn't the case with my birth family. It seemed their connection was of blood, not of love.

The gravity of the situation had started to sink in. Less than a week before, none of these people were in my life. It was a bit like an out-of-body experience. Sometimes it felt like I watched it all go down as a bystander. It's crazy that with one phone call, I had five new people in my life, a mother, an aunt, a sister, a brother, and a cousin, with many more to meet. The whole thing was crazy. After eating snacks and drinking a little port, the group started slowing down; we shared our lives and photos of important or interesting events. The evening ended much too soon when Debi, Dolores, and Diane all left for the evening. I'm sure they were exhausted from all the emotions as well.

It was time to be alone with Vicki and Mike in our suite. We spent the next several hours eating, drinking wine, and talking nonstop. I heard stories from their childhoods; neither was particularly happy, but it was informative. Although we were all interested in each other's stories, I hung on every word. Even though the consensus was that Diane wasn't a great mom, I listened to the stories with an open mind. I wanted to have a relationship with her without being tainted by others' opinions. I wanted to decide who she was in the world from what she put into our relationship rather than assume the negative. My perspective differed from anyone else's, which would make a difference in my relationship with her. She's older and hopefully wiser and will look at our relationship separately from the others, who all seem to have animosity toward her.

I had shared my adoption papers with Mike already but not yet with Vicki. So the evening continued with the three of us speculating about what may have happened in the months and years around our births. Even though I was the new one in the trio, Vicki and Mike didn't know each other well either, so this created an excellent opportunity for me to feel like I was on a similar footing with them both. We all got comfy, and I loved having the chance to sit in my jammies, drink a glass of wine and listen to them talk. As I listened, I thought about how sad it was that they were separated when they were young.

Some additional tidbits came out over wine that night. It sounded like Fred, Vicki's stepfather, had physically and sexually abused all three girls. So many thoughts went through my mind after hearing about the abuse. Did Diane know? How could she not know? No wonder the youngest girls have nothing to do with their mom if she had known and didn't support them. That would be a tough pill to swallow if she had looked the other way. They told stories about how money was always a topic of conversation, and there was never enough. Diane worked two and three jobs most of her married life to make ends meet. Mike and Vicki were convinced she stayed with her abusive husband because of his Naval pension. She was only looking to give herself a more comfortable life later when she retired. She would have their social security, whichever was higher, and his Navy pension.

We could have talked all night, but we grudgingly decided to go to bed when the clock was about to strike midnight. I was emotionally exhausted after this eventful day. So much new information, and so many emotions, overload for sure.

The Next Day

I woke up after sleeping better than I had for the last several nights. The anxiety of our meeting had melted away, and I slept like a baby. I felt comfortable with my new family and looked forward to the future. I remember just waking up; I sat up in bed and thought, "I can't imagine our reunion going any better." I had tried to keep my expectations low so I wouldn't be disappointed, but it had gone amazingly well. I reflected on the day and felt very blessed. No hidden agendas came out that I couldn't handle; just several strangers came together to open their lives to each other. When I think of those reflections, I was relieved no one got drunk or angry like my family.

Mike, Vicki, and I all had a slow relaxing start to our day; I joined my sister and brother right back where we were the night before. The only difference was I had a cup of coffee in my hand instead of a glass of wine. We continued to talk openly about ourselves, our families, and our lives. It was very comforting to pull my legs up under my bathrobe and feel the warmth of my coffee. I didn't worry whether my hair was sticking out or my breath was terrible. I felt completely accepted for who I was, a very nice feeling indeed. After a couple of hours, Vicki's attention started to wander back to California and her five-hour drive home. We got ready for the day and headed out. I was disappointed Vicki needed to make the drive so soon, but I asked her specifically how she saw the future unfolding for us. She was sweet, said she wanted to keep in touch, and would like me to meet her husband, kids, and grandkids. Her life was entrenched in Northern California, so I hoped to drive down in the next six months to meet her family and share more time with her. We said our goodbyes with hugs and well wishes, and she returned to her life in California. My husband and I have since visited

Vicki and her family numerous times as we've made our way from Oregon to California.

After Vicki left, Mike & I called Diane and said we would be there shortly to take her to breakfast. We shared a nice meal, and I continued filling in the blanks in some stories. Then, we returned to Diane's apartment and sat around her table, looking at a few more photos she had pulled out for us to see.

I especially liked this photo of her in her early twenties and the second one in her late 30s or early 40s. I could see some similarities in our features.

During our time together, my mom showed me some of her hobbies. She crocheted and knitted just like I do. I found these similarities fascinating and always looked for anything that connected us. Before I left this initial visit, she gave me a crocheted lap blanket, a scarf, and a hat set for myself and my daughter Chelsey. I had brought her a gift too, a thank you gesture I hoped she would like. I gave her a collection of my photographs, butterflies, and flowers in a book I had assembled the previous year. I wrote a little note to thank her for the chance to get to know her.

When I got home from Bend, I spent a lot of time reflecting on the experience and my new relatives. One thing didn't sit well. It was how Loni, the youngest sister, had been AWOL for the last 20 years, and no one had looked for her. So I figured I'd look for her and see what I found. I did a quick search on the internet, and I found her almost immediately. Instead of reaching out to her directly, I thought it best to be respectful to my new family and tell Vicki about finding Loni and let her reach out. Vicki wrote Loni a letter and, in her correspondence, said to her that their mom had another daughter, and I had been adopted out. Because of her history with her family, Loni wasn't quite as anxious to re-engage as I had been to meet her. It took her a few weeks to answer Vicki's letter, but when she did, Vicki gave her my phone number so we could connect. In fact, when I got the initial call from Loni, we talked for over two hours. I was in my car, parked in a parking garage, and didn't budge until the conversation ended. We both agreed we wanted to meet, but she was in Arizona, and I was in Oregon. We decided if she would go on a road trip in a couple weeks, she could stay with my husband and me in our spare room. That would give us lots of time to get to know each other. Besides getting to know me, Mike lived a few miles away, so she could reconnect with him. Loni had only met Mike one time when Loni was about 11 and Mike was in his early 20s.

Loni drove from Chandler, AZ, to Portland a couple weeks later. It was a great couple of weeks. We drove all around the metro area; we talked and laughed until my face hurt. Mike and Loni had a similar sense of humor and a negative view of the world, so they hit it off well. I'm more of a Pollyanna type, usually finding the bright side to even the worst situation. Being the connector I am, I asked Loni if she was interested in seeing her mom again. Since it had been 20 years since Loni had seen her mom or sisters, I hoped she could find a way to open her heart. At first, Loni wasn't interested in rekindling any relationship with her mom. She went on to tell us stories of growing up with her mom and Fred. She had nothing good to say about her dad. Instead of calling him dad, she bitterly called him her "sperm donor." Loni described how all the girls had been sexually abused by Fred. Loni told her mom of the abuse at some point, and unfortunately for the girls, she didn't believe it had happened and sided with their father. The bitterness and pain were evident all these years later. Forgiveness wasn't in her vocabulary. All I could think of was, "I missed that bullet." My growing up was no picnic, but I wasn't sexually abused by my adopted parents as a child. When Loni left after two weeks of staying with us in Oregon, I didn't know when we would see each other again. That afternoon, we heard from her; her car had broken down in Boise, and Mike was on the way to pick her up and bring her back to our house, getting the vehicle towed back with her. Luckily, it wasn't a problem for us, and by the time she left for real a week later, she had decided to move back to the Pacific NW.

In 2009 after their move back to Oregon, we started doing things together. My husband and I spent a lot of time socially with Mike, Loni, and her husband. We rode motorcycles and snowmobiles together; we went camping and just hung out at each other's homes. We had lots of fun and made some great memories. My favorite trip was when we all went to Diamond Lake in the winter. The lake was frozen solid. With Mike's encouragement, we all walked out on the frozen lake and got a completely different view of the area. We ate, drank, and laughed in between riding the snowmobiles and finding other mischief to get into.

The highlight of our trip happened when we all rode our snowmobiles from Diamond Lake to Crater Lake in pristine snow. It was gorgeous. The only way to see Crater Lake in the winter is by snowmobile; the access is closed to cars in the winter since they don't plow. It had snowed several inches the night before, so the snow was untouched. The sun was out, so the snow sparkled like diamonds.

Crater Lake with Loni and Her Husband

We made the very first tracks from one lake to the other. The contrast of the deep blue of the lake, the blue of the sky, and the snow was breathtaking. It was truly magical. Crater Lake is gorgeous if you haven't ever experienced it in the summer, but it is spectacular in the winter under these conditions.

Another fun memory from 2010 was when Mike and I visited Vicki's retirement party in California. Vicki worked for the school system for many years, and we were excited to celebrate her

Crater Lake with Mike, Loni, and David

retirement at a great little restaurant near her home. Her retirement was in January, so Mike & I planned the trip hoping the weather would hold for the drive. We were fortunate that the trip over the Siskiyou's was uneventful. The retirement party was fun, and we all drank too much. But Mike was the funniest. I remember him literally holding up the wall with the goofiest expression on his face. He didn't feel very good the following day after all those shots.

Camping together was a fun way for all of us to spend time together. I have never seen anybody take so much stuff camping. Loni & David were equipped to stay a month. They took everything they could possibly need and much more, considering we only stayed a few days. But, again, we laughed, talked, shared food and drink, and made wonderful memories.

I continued to make occasional trips across the mountain to visit Diane. We got closer and closer. Then, her health started to deteriorate, along with her memory. Unfortunately, the closer Mike and Loni got, the more challenging it was for Mike to spend time with Diane. It was like he had to pick sides. He started referring to Diane as Mother Dearest. One trip, I asked if Mike and Loni wanted to go, and shockingly, they both decided to make the trip with me to Bend.

Unfortunately, I think that trip was the beginning of the end for my relationship with Mike and Loni. By the end of the visit, Loni was belligerent and argumentative, and that was the last time Loni saw or talked to our mom. Mike had chosen sides that weren't his mom's or mine. I wanted to maintain a relationship with all of them if possible. Diane's health was growing more fragile with each trip. She had a triple bypass surgery and breast cancer before I met her. Now her rib bones were crumbling from osteoporosis where they had opened her up. Her doctor had placed two metal plates with 48 screws in her chest to hold her ribs together after her open-heart surgery, and now they were slipping. Every time she coughed or sneezed, it was painful. She would hold a pillow up and squeeze it to support her chest. Soon after our initial visit, she was put on oxygen 24/7 for COPD; each time I visited, she was frailer than the last. It didn't feel like she would last much longer, but she was tougher than I knew.

Social times with Mike, Loni, and her husband were more limited after that trip to Bend. I tried to keep in touch, but the effort seemed one-sided. So, I stopped trying as hard. Perhaps when Diane was gone, I could reconnect with Loni and Mike. But for now, those relationships seemed a bit strained.

Cari was the last sister for me to meet. She had heard from Vicki about me but didn't want to have a relationship. But the second time I made the trip down to California to visit Vicki,

Vicky, Cari, and Me

she reached out to Cari and said we were all going to dinner and asked her to join us, and she did.

She was nice enough, and I was thankful she was willing to meet me. Since that first dinner, we have gone to dinner a couple more times, and once, she brought her daughter and granddaughter along for us to meet. We're friends on Facebook, but I doubt we will ever have a real relationship. I visit Vicki about once a year or two when we visit grandkids in California. But, again, it seemed like I was making most of the effort, so I have backed off some with her too.

DNA Testing

DNA has the power to change people's lives and their history. Compassion and understanding must be practiced for ourselves and those who came before us. Our ancestors, great-grandparents, grandparents, and even our parents lived in vastly different times where a judgment of past mistakes was commonplace. So many people hid those missteps to avoid feeling judged. Those missteps could potentially put a black cloud over the person who committed the error in judgment and their entire family. The shame brought down on an unwed mother was palpable. Becoming pregnant with another man's child was vehemently denied. These blunders or love stories are the fabric of every family's history and can change the trajectory of lives, especially when secrets are revealed. These births were often recorded incorrectly, hiding the birthfather's identity, thus changing the family story without the family knowing the truth.

Some of these secrets remained buried for generations until the technology of DNA revealed the truth. These tests have changed the facts as we know them and have brought to light their unique situations. DNA's information may answer many questions but tends to leave us with many more questions. DNA has brought family stories out of the dark and into the light. By doing so, the truth is revealed, but that truth can break trust, shatter beliefs, and rewrite history. By opening the door to DNA results, you may discover the answers to questions you have had for many years. Chances are you will open a can of worms, unraveling family stories that have existed for decades. It's important to be open to these changing stories. Some of these stories were put in place to save face or to avoid public shame. Some were put in place to make life easier for those involved. I'm sure they all seemed like a good idea at the time. I believe we all do our best, but sometimes our choices cause chaos in our lives and those of others.

I decided it was time to bite the bullet and get my DNA done in 2017. I'd had an account on Ancestry.com for several years after I found my birth mother. After I got the DNA test results, I had many matches, but DNA is complicated. I didn't know what to do with all this information. So I went to Bend to share my DNA results with Diane. I pulled out my computer and shared some exciting parts like nationality. We don't have access to this information when a person is adopted, so I was excited to find out where my ancestors were from. On St Patrick's Day, I told people I was Irish, but honestly, I didn't have proof I had any Irish blood in me until now. I shared with my birth mom that I was 35% Scottish, 28 % Irish,

5% Welsh, and 26% English. I was excited to show her, and she was intrigued with the Ancestry platform and all the information available. I could tell her facts about her relatives she had forgotten, like names of relatives, when they were born, married, and died. It was a good refresher for her and opened new conversations for us.

I'd been told that if I could locate a male relative and get their DNA, I could identify my birth father. So soon after returning from Bend, I reached out to Scott, one of Loni's sons, and told him what I needed and that I was willing to pay for his Ancestry DNA test. I dropped the test off at his home and waited for the results. Unfortunately, I didn't understand what to do, so it wasn't particularly helpful.

A month later, my husband & I decided to take a road trip from Oregon to Utah. Our friends have a home in Salt Lake and another in Moab. I have always wanted to see and photograph Southern Utah, so we would make it happen. So, in our whirlwind fashion, we called our friends, and they were thrilled to hear from us. They planned on being home and invited us to come to their home. We were on the road to Utah in two days. While in Salt Lake, we stopped at the Family History Center, the Mormon genealogy center. I talked to the sweetest couple about how I was looking for the identity of my birth father. The young man revealed that he was on the same quest for his dad, who was also adopted. He explained since my bio mom was still alive if I got her DNA, I could compare my matches on ancestry and determine which ones were hers; the rest would be my bio fathers.

I was pumped. I got on Ancestry and ordered a new test, which was delivered when I got home from our Utah trip. After returning to Oregon, I made a quick trip to Bend with my new DNA kit. The funny thing was that I hadn't mentioned the test to Diane, but she had been thinking about the results I showed her since my last visit. When I got there, practically the first thing she talked about was the information I had shown her on Ancestry.com. She had been so excited by what I had shown her she wanted to have me do the test for her. I giggled as I intended to find my father with her DNA information, and she was more interested in her heritage breakdown. Either way, I was getting her to spit in the small vial, and we would accomplish both with one test. If I could find my birth father, my life would change yet again.

Several weeks passed, and Diane's DNA integrated with mine automatically, giving me more complex information. I wasn't sure what to do with it all, but I had faith I'd figure it out. I was visiting a friend in Las Vegas in December when I got a crazy phone call. Her name was Jody; she said she was related to my stepdaughter Breanna. We had communicated some through Ancestry messaging and then by email. I had told her about the DNA test my mom had done and my desire to figure out my birth father's identity. She offered to help me with my search. Seriously? I had a search angel. Jody explained centimorgans to me and sent me a chart to determine their meaning and what to do with them. Half of what she said was over my head, but she has been studying genealogy for over 30 years. I was so grateful she was willing to share what she knew. I felt blessed she had reached out to me, and the timing was incredible. Jody then looked at my DNA matches and figured out which were from my mom's side and which were from my father's. It was like magic. She then triangulated which branch of my ancestors my birth father came from. She suggested I look through a particular line to identify my bio dad. If you have ever gone through the hints on Ancestry and tried to stay on track, it can be tricky and very easy to go down a rabbit hole. I remember sitting on my comfy chair going through all these people, and Wham!! A lightning bolt just jumped off my computer. I found my birth father. There he was in black and white. OMG, I found him. I was all alone, and screaming or jumping up and down seemed silly, but I needed that energy to go somewhere. Who could I call? Who could I tell? I couldn't believe it. I found him. His name was Jacques O'Keefe. Unfortunately, I also found out he had died in

Photo by Bryant, Nampa

MR. AND MRS. MICHAEL J. O'KEEFE
Nieves Arano weds Portland Man

1990. Bummer. I called Jody, told her her suggestion worked and found him. So there he was a Portland, OR. police officer in 1953, just like my bio mom had said. In fact, Jody let me use her account to find a few newspaper articles to enhance my search. So I did some research and found two articles with photographs of him. The first was a wedding photo in the Nampa, Idaho newspaper from the spring of 1950. There he was, smiling, standing by his new wife, young, dark-haired, handsome, ready to cut the cake. Then I found another photo, this one from the Oregonian. He got his police badge for the Portland Police Department in October of 1950. Wow! Jackpot. Jacque is the one shaking the hand of the chief.

He was featured in the photo getting his badge; what a longshot.

In one day, I found my birthfather and two photos of him. The reality that I would never meet him hit me hard, but when I found pictures, that helped. I also found a long article without a photo of him. This time the article

was about his life with his second wife, Audrey. She had been a teacher for 50 years, and the article highlighted her life, her contributions to the community throughout the 30 years she married Jacques, and their plans after retirement. By the end of the next day, I had also found my bio father's widow in Augusta, GA. Before I called her, I prayed she was alive and willing to talk to me. The first number I called was disconnected. I found a second one and dialed that number before I lost my nerve. My mind was racing; how should I introduce myself? Should I tell her right from the beginning?

She answered, and I introduced myself to Audrey and asked if I had caught her at a good time. I didn't beat around the bush; I just told her. I explained my search for my birth father from my DNA results; Jacques O'Keefe was my birth father. I explained how I found my birth mother in 2008. I told her I had done my DNA test this year through Ancestry.com and recently got my mom's DNA test. She never questioned me or doubted what I told her. I asked her some questions, and we hung up after two hours and nine pages of notes.

She told me about my grandparents, which was so cool. Jacques's father, my grandfather, was known as Pop. John Sr was Catholic; his wife was Methodist. My grandfather worked in the coal mines in Iowa, and Maxine, Jacque's mom, would take him lunch daily. Jacques's parents lived in a house a few blocks from the railroad tracks. It ran so regularly; they could set their clock by it. Jacques's mom had smoked a lot through the years and had terrible lungs. Pop would stop at the pub most every day after work which didn't go over well with his wife. Maxine served supper every day promptly at 5:30pm and expected Pop to be home for dinner on time. If he stayed at the pub too long, which he did way too often, she didn't get mad; he just ate a lot of cold food for dinner.

Pop learned to fly before WWII as a young man. He was an officer in the war, where he taught others to fly. He also spent time at Avenger Field in Texas, teaching the women in WAF to fly. Part of his responsibilities was to fly out supplies to soldiers. Jacques always wanted his dad to teach him to fly, but he never would. Pop stopped in Portland to get refueled frequently. He loved the area so much that he moved his family there. He returned to Portland and built a house for his parents before 1950 so they would also move to the NW.

She also told me about her younger years. Audrey grew up and lived in Yonkers, NY, and attended NW University. This was during the Korean War. She had been engaged but broke it off and decided to take a job in Portland, OR, to teach first grade. She reflected on when she and Jacques met and moved forward with their relationship. Audrey met Jacques the night his divorce was final (5/5/54). Jacques was a Portland motorcycle police officer. Audrey and her friends danced at a popular downtown bar with excellent dance music. They met that night. I'm unsure if he was on duty at the time. Their first official date was three days later, and he introduced her to his parents the same day. After that, she saw him on and off for the next several months. She said he would drive by the house on his on-duty days to ensure she was safe; on his off-duty days, he would have one of his police buddies go by. Today that sounds like being stalked, but she liked the feeling of security.

In 1955 Jacques and Audrey went to Reno for the July 4th holiday with her best friend and husband. She remembered Jacques brought up getting married over the holiday. He joked, "If we got married here, we'd have to keep it a secret." That sounded like he assumed they would marry. Jacques was in the Army reserves during this time, so they had obligations to complete. She talked about a couple other trips they went on, including one to Hawaii. They both loved to travel. Audrey didn't think he was

mature enough for her to marry then, so she left
Portland and took a teaching job in Las Vegas.
They talked over the phone for over a year after
she moved. He had said he was a good cop but
quit the police department because of the poor
treatment of minorities, and he wouldn't get
involved in that behavior. He eventually
followed her to Las Vegas and bartended at the
Frontier Bar for a while. They reunited and
started dating again in the spring of 1957. He
proposed very quickly after that, but Audrey
gave him several conditions he needed to agree
to before she would agree to marry him. She
said she would continue to teach through the
end of the school year in June, and then she
would quit teaching for a while. They had to
marry in NY, so her family was present. He
"had to get his act together, have no bills, buy a
ring, and have $1000 saved." I loved this; she
was a tough cookie who knew what she wanted.
She needed him to grow up and take
responsibility if he would marry her. I never
asked her what that meant exactly, but I guess
his wandering eye may have had something to
do with her demands.

He must have agreed because they married Dec 28, 1957, in Stamford, CT, West Chester County. This was an affluent area about 30 miles from Yonkers, where they loved to ski together. She said Jacques was an excellent skier. She went home to NY for that Christmas and most of the Christmas after that, even if Jacques couldn't go as she was close to her family. They came home to spend New Year's Eve with Jacques' family and moved back to Portland shortly after. Jacques served in the Army reserves and worked out of Fort Lewis, WA.

Jacques returned to active duty on March 6, 1967, for the Vietnam War, so Audrey lived in Army housing while he was gone. He went to Si Pan on a ship whose mission was to bring dead soldiers back from the front line. He was also assigned to North Japan to spy on the Russians. He finally learned to fly even if it wasn't his father instructing him. She waitressed for a while and used her tips to learn to fly too. He flew around the Caribbean, spying on Russians around Sputnik time. Some of his duties included listening to Russian communication signals and jamming them so they couldn't be received.

He received honors from the Army Security Agency for his time in Vietnam. During the early years of conflict, ASA troops were assigned to the 3rd Radio Research Unit. Their primary mission was to locate Viet Cong transmitters operating in the south. He also ran the R and R camp in Vietnam. When he went to war, we weighed 210; when he returned, he had no hair and weighed 140 lbs. In 1968 alone, he had a bad flu and almost died.

During their time off, they rented a plane and flew 28 days around the US. They both loved to travel and did so as often as they could. This month-long trip was an excellent highlight during so much turmoil in the late '60s.

After the war ended, Jacques went to San Francisco, CA, to learn how to make dentures for other service members. After that, his colonel told him, "I have two things to tell you, you aren't going back to Japan, and you're moving to New Mexico for more schooling." The school principal of a New Mexico elementary school called Audrey and said, "We need you here in seven days; we have 35 sixth graders waiting for you." They drove their VW bug across the country and drove night and day to arrive on time. In their six years in New Mexico, Audrey got her master's degree and loved being back to teaching. Jacques spent time in the White Sands Missile Range in New Mexico, where the Army tested rockets and missiles. He went back into dentistry at Fort Devens, MA, after that. When they were at Fort Devens, he struggled with his health. They also had the opportunity to spend six years in Europe; he was the head of a dental lab run by the Department of Defense, among a few other odd jobs.

Jacques was a great bowler, and he liked to play golf. He ran tournaments for both. Unfortunately, he drank and smoked, contributing to his early demise at 61. They had no children but enjoyed having dogs and cats most of their lives. They moved to Atlanta to open his dental lab when he retired from the Army. After six years, he was called to supervise a group in Augusta. He lived with

Audrey and their animals the rest of his life in Augusta, GA.

In February 1990, he got severely ill; his heart valve stopped working in March. He was in rehab until June to get stronger and then had surgery in July to repair his heart with pig guts, then he was on oxygen. But unfortunately, he didn't feel well the day after Thanksgiving, went to the hospital, and never got out. He died on 12/16/1990.

He had a standard military funeral. Jacques was buried in North Yonkers near Hudson. Hastings on Hudson under Audrey's family tree, where her mom and dad were buried. Audrey and I talked in 2017, and she told me she walked with a cane and a walker; she turned 86 on Dec 26, 2017.

She'll be buried next to Jacques under that tree when the time comes. I couldn't believe how much information she would share with me. I sat there in shock; my first inclination was to jump on an airplane and fly from Portland, OR across the country to Augusta, GA, to spend more time with her. I would have loved to go through her photo albums and go down memory lane even more than she already had. I never met her; she may be gone by now, but I felt so blessed I had this opportunity to get so much firsthand information about her life with my birth father.

Jacques First Wife

Audrey couldn't help me too much with Jacques' first wife, Nieve, and his boys. But here's what she did know. Nieve Arano was born between Spain and France in the small country of Basque. She and her family moved to Nampa, Idaho, and she married Jacques in 1950 after serving in WWII as a nurse. She and Jacques had two sons, and they were separated more than they were together through their volatile marriage.

From what I could gather, his first wife, Nieve, left Portland and returned to Nampa, Idaho, where her parents lived in 1954. Jacques supported the boys after she moved, but Nieve wouldn't allow him to see his boys after their split. Audrey remembers Jacques talking about getting the boys a swing set for Christmas one year after the divorce.

Unfortunately, she wouldn't allow him to see the boys when he tried to deliver it, even with gifts. I believe the marriage was annulled since she was Catholic and wanted to remarry. However, per the archdiocese, there should be legal state papers of divorce which I found even if it was annulled in the church. She later married Henry Jones in 1958 and was thrilled to have a good man raise her boys. Jacques continued to pay support for a while with support bonds but stopped when it was clear he wouldn't ever be able to see the boys. She thought the boys' names were Patrick and Michael, two of the most popular Irish names imaginable.

Looking for Jacques' Boys

I knew about the boys, but it would be tricky to find Michael and Patrick O'Keefe, their father's name, or Jones, their stepfather's name. When I looked at the obituaries, I realized some details were wrong. Jacques' first wife had two sisters, not just one. Nieve died in 1979 of ovarian cancer. Her sister Vivian and Marie died many years after her, but their obituaries were very helpful in finding more information about Nieves's boys. From these documents, I discovered their stepfather's name, Henry Jones. Also, they lived in several cities around Sacramento, CA. I determined their middle names from Ancestry using approximate birthdates and where they might live.

I found several phone numbers and addresses for Patrick Shawn Jones and Michael Patrick Jones, so I started down that path. I left several messages, and a few days later, I got a call back from Jean Jones, Patrick's wife. She started by saying I had the wrong number but, within a few moments, realized we were talking about the same person. Unfortunately, Patrick had died four years before. She was very gracious to talk to me and told me a bit about Patrick and Michael. She shared a cell number for Michael; that was my next contact. I texted him but didn't hear anything, so over the weekend, I called. I left him a message, but he didn't return my call or the text. I've thought a lot about my bio father, a police officer who abused his power in the 50s. He may have taken advantage of many women he pulled over for traffic offenses. Looking back on women's rights and society's message, women were merely their husband's property. In fact, it was not until 1968, when the civil rights amendment was ratified, that women were legally considered equals. While looking at the law, it appeared to be an afterthought even in 1968. Discrimination due to sex was first mentioned on the 2nd to the last page of this 38-page document. It was stated twice in two paragraphs, which changed the course of history for all of us. This amendment gave women the same rights as African American men and women in 1968.

In the early '50s, the Portland, Oregon, police department was corrupt. Several books have been written about the payoffs and those blatantly ignoring the law for personal benefit. Luckily, I have not found my bio father's name in any of those books, but it explains the times and situation better. Women felt powerless. Women used their sexual attractiveness to solve an immediate problem, like being stopped for drunk driving. Police officers obliged the women's need to be released from the financial burden and legal consequences of a DUI, so they struck a deal. How often did that happen? It happened to my birth mom; I am sure she was not the only one who paid this price for her poor judgment of impaired driving.

Did the women understand that this was a way to solve their legal problems? The decision to have sex with a police officer caused my biological mom to deal with an unwanted pregnancy and the loss of her son to her ex-husband. His behavior, whether this or another indiscretion, affected his first wife and their boys drastically. There are no innocent people in these scenarios.

Unless we lived in those times and could wear their shoes, it isn't easy to fully understand the motivation of the men or the women. It does make me wonder if the police targeted young women for this purpose. Maybe, but we will never know for sure. Because of my conception, my birth father did not take his marriage vows seriously. As the story unfolds, he ultimately loses his wife and two boys and possibly his career in law enforcement because of his actions. All the decisions we make have consequences, whether it is 1953 or today. We have all done things we are not proud of and have paid dearly for many of those choices. That is one reason it's not my place to be my bio mom or dad's judge or jury. They lived out their self-induced punishment and, in many cases, have taken it to their graves.

Jacques was inducted into the police force in 1950 but left the police force in 1955. I went to the archives in Portland, OR, where an old city employee's employment records are stored, and I got a photo attached to his records. From his records, I also found that he was suspended in 1954 for "behavior not conducive to a police officer." This coincides with his wife filing for divorce. His divorce was final in May of 1954. He then left the force a year later. My guess, the behavior that got him suspended happened again, and he was asked to resign. After leaving the police force, he followed Audrey to Las Vegas in 1956 and applied for a police officer position at the Las Vegas Police Department but was denied. Whatever he did, the LVPD didn't want his behavior there either. So I guess he got caught on at least two occasions with his pants down or from the consequences of those actions.

Another Brother?

In 2018 I decided to visit a friend in Connecticut for a couple days before I went to New York to spend time with my daughter. My friend and her husband took me on a short road trip so I could see the area around their home. While we were driving, the subject of my birth parents came up, and I told them both the story that had unfolded so far, the cliff notes version, and Rick said he had also done some research on his ancestors. He was excited to share some of what he had found, so as soon as we got home, we pulled out our computers to share the details. I opened my Ancestry account to the DNA area to explain how I could pinpoint who my bio father was. I got off the couch to show Rick, and I saw it. There was a new person on the first page of my matches. Not only was he on the first page, but he was also between my half-brother Mike and my half-sister Vicki. How could that be? I looked at the centimorgans, and we shared 1762 centimorgans. That meant he was likely another half-brother but this time on my father's side. I immediately sent him a message through Ancestry. I was anxious to find out who this mystery person could be. While waiting for a message, I went onto Facebook and LinkedIn to see what I could find. I typed his name in and found several men with the same name. I messaged a few of them and asked if they had done their DNA recently. I noticed one who lived in Portland and thought how cool it would be if he were my relative.

I got up the following day and looked at my phone. There was a Facebook message from the new person on my Ancestry dashboard. I opened the message, and he said, yes, he had done the DNA, and he had noticed my name on the top of his matches as well. He finished his message with a simple sentence, "I'll call you tomorrow afternoon." That was today. I had a reservation on a bus that went between Hartford, CT, and New York City at 3:30pm. With the three-hour time difference, I could hear from him anytime. I felt a bit anxious when I boarded the bus for my trip to NY. About an hour into the trip, my phone rang; it was a Portland number. I answered it, trying to whisper since it was quiet on the bus.

Since I reached out initially, I felt it was my place to start the conversation. Here goes. I gave him the short version of how I had just found my birth father a few weeks before, and it appeared Tim was on my birth father's DNA string. He asked my birth father's name, and when I told him, his first reaction was to laugh. He explained that he was raised by his mom and a stepdad, and only in the last few years had he heard the name of his biological father. He had asked his mom several times through the years, but she had refused to say for sure who his bio father was until she was close to her own death. His mom finally told him, and Jacques O'Keefe was the name she had spoken of. I told him the little I knew about him thus far. I explained how I was conceived, and then we ended the call. I didn't want to hang up, but being on a bus was awkward. It wasn't ten minutes later when I realized I had so many more questions, and if I didn't get some answers, I would burst. I started to text him; I hoped I wasn't intruding. Over text, I was able to get a few more details, like where he worked for 20 years and how he had recently retired. The more I thought about the fact that he had lived in Portland all these years, the more I hoped I hadn't dated the guy unknowingly, ooo ick. I had to find out where he went to school and his marital situation. Luckily, it was a quiet Sunday afternoon, and the answers came right back. At the end of our communications, I suggested I reach out as soon as I got home from my trip.

Meeting Tim, My Half Brother

I was home a couple of days before I reached out to Tim. I wanted us to get together for lunch in the next few days if possible. I threw it out there in a text and waited for an answer. It was several hours before I got a return text, but to my surprise, it wasn't from Tim; it was from his oldest daughter on his phone. She explained that her dad was excited to meet me, but she needed to explain what was going on in their lives. While I was in NY, Tim suffered a mild stroke. He was being treated at Emanuel Hospital in Portland, OR, and would be released to rehab soon. He was having trouble with his right side, especially his leg. It would take physical therapy to get his full mobility back. When Tim entered the emergency a few days before, the doctors did a battery of tests to diagnose the stroke and document the extent of the damage. Unfortunately, when the test results were analyzed, they found more than stroke damage; they found a cancerous mass on his lung and several spots elsewhere. After several texts back and forth with his daughter, we decided that today was a great time for me to meet him and both of his daughters. I got on my shoes and headed to Emanuel Hospital.

All the way there, I felt a bit anxious, wondering how the meeting would go, but I had an overall good feeling. I wondered if there was any resemblance, if they would accept me, or if this would be my only meeting. As I walked into his hospital room, all my fears melted away. Kristy, the oldest daughter I had been texting with, jumped up immediately as I entered the room. With tears in her eyes, she gave me a huge hug. The younger sister Amanda waited patiently for her turn. All the while I was hugging the girls, I could see Tim with a big smile on his face sitting on the edge of the bed, waiting patiently to talk to me.

We hugged, and it was like we had known each other forever. After the initial pleasantries, I explained the exceptionally long story of our birth father. I explained how I found out he was my birth father and how he had met my birth mother. I told him about my research and the hours I had explored Ancestry and other platforms. I also told him about my conversation with Audrey, our father's widow in Georgia. He briefly told me about how his mom had told him his father was actually his stepfather while he was in high school. He explained how angry, confused, and hurt he was by the news. It was a blow, but it worsened when his mom didn't tell him anything else about him. After many more years, he finally got his name but never knew more than that. He assumed that he and his mom had a brief affair because she married his stepfather shortly after his birth. Just like me, Jacques probably never knew he existed.

I spent four hours in the hospital for our first encounter. While I was there, Tim's half-sister on his mom's side also came to visit. She told me later how sad she was when she considered visiting her brother at the hospital. While walking down the hallway, she was surprised to hear laughter coming out of his room. She walked in and joined the party. Patty was born in 1955, and our birthdays are only one day apart. She told me more about herself and her son, including how she had suffered a mild

Visiting Tim in the Hospital

stroke a few years before. Tim shared some childhood stories and how he was an artist and musician and traveled as a younger man with several rock n roll bands.

Tim and His Girls

He talked about how hard it was not knowing anything about his biological father and his mom not being willing to give him any details. Shortly after our initial visit, Tim was moved into a rehab center. I had several opportunities to visit and get to know him and his close family. Unfortunately, shortly after entering rehab, he got the test results that would change the course of his life. No one had guessed how sick he was until the news revealed he had terminal cancer. Tim was diagnosed with stage four lung cancer and was given three-six months to live. The shock was overwhelming, but denial crept in as well. I have known many people with stage four cancer, mainly breast cancer, but they lived many years because of treatments. The stark reality came when we all attended the family meeting with the palliative care doctors. Tim had made the decision not to do any treatment at all. He would only agree to a few simple measures to keep him comfortable as the pain increased. I was able to ask a few questions and found that even if he did aggressive treatment, it would only improve life expectancy by a few months. I resigned myself, as did his girls; Tim would most likely lose his battle in 2018.

When Tim returned home, I visited several times. I communicated with his daughters mostly because Tim was struggling with the side effects of the stroke. He was depressed with his limitations and the reality of the cancer news. Tim had been very independent, so he struggled with needing help. Hospice was set up, and a schedule was established. When I visited, he always said he was doing fine, which I knew he wasn't. He put on a brave face for me and others that loved him. Unfortunately, Tim

Celebrating His 66th Birthday

withdrew emotionally and went downhill very quickly. He shut down when he realized this was his life. The exception was his birthday.

In April, his girls threw Tim a great 66th birthday party. I met some of his friends and relatives that came to celebrate his last birthday. I got to know him a little better from other people's perspectives.

Tim and His Girls

Timing is Everything.

I was out of town when I realized Tim was declining rapidly. Tim's brother Mike and his sister Patty were at the house when I returned. The family dynamics were uncomfortable. By this time, he wasn't communicating; he wasn't eating or drinking anything, so I knew it was just a matter of time. I was able to be there four days of the last six. I look at my time with him as a gift from God. I had struggled and asked myself, "Why was I brought into this mix during the last few months of Tim's life." Reflecting on that question, I felt I was brought into Tim's life for closure around his birth father. I was able to give him answers to questions he needed to die in peace. I was able to spend those hard days with his girls and hopefully offer them some strength during this challenging time. I was there to help them with their dads' transition and hopefully continue being in their lives. During the last week of Tim's life, the family dynamics started to change drastically.

I heard stories from Tim's life I hadn't heard yet. He loved music; he was a musician and worked at The Blues Festival in Portland for over 20 years. He was an incredible artist, drawing both realistic and stylized. He was incredibly talented; I'm sorry I didn't get to know that man before he died. I also heard about the downside of the music business that many musicians fall into. He had a heroin addiction. His oldest brother died from a heroin overdose, and his younger brother was an addict as well. Several other relationships were highly strained, and some crumbled under stress. I cherished those tough days to be able to help, support the girls, and give them a few hours of respite.

During this time of transition, there were so many emotions, memories, and regrets to process. Because I wasn't involved in the years of drama, I was able to be more objective and help with some of the emotions others were trying to avoid. When someone fades slowly, it brings unprocessed emotions from the past to the forefront. Many people stuff years of conflict and unprocessed emotions come to the surface with the stress of death. This can be very unexpected and uncomfortable, creating volatile reactions in family members. Being the new element in this family, everyone was on their best behavior, but as soon as I left, it turned ugly with guilt, insecurities, and anger. We lost Tim five months after our initial meeting, but I continue to check in with his daughters.

It Happened Again

I visited my bio mom Diane in Bend after the snow subsided in the spring of 2018. I printed out her information so she could show it to her sister and discuss their DNA. I wanted to show her mine again so we could compare. I pulled out the computer, and there she was - another close relative, Tiffany. I was excited to see where this led me, so I immediately wrote to her and hoped she would write back soon. The following day, sure enough, she wrote me back, and we were related. Her dad was another half-brother on my father's side. We scheduled a time to talk, and during that conversation, I realized I had another half-brother and a sister. Dennis was born Feb 13,1956, and his sister Tana was born Apr 14, 1957. Unfortunately, Jacques wasn't a father to either of these children and left their lives shortly after Tana's birth. When I compared the dates with what Audrey had told me, Jacques had left to follow Audrey to Las Vegas shortly after her birth. This story is getting messier all the time.

Tiffany, my new niece, told me that her grandma, Elayne, was 16 or 17 when she and

Jacques were together and had her dad. The timing dictates that around May of 1955, they got together. Jacques left his job in October 1955, about the time she would have known about her pregnancy, and perhaps she was the reason he left the police department. This was also when Audrey moved to Las Vegas and wasn't with him other than on phone calls. Seems like he constantly needed a woman in his life.

The relationship with a minor may be why Jacques "left" his job and decided to move to Las Vegas. Two children later with an underage girl, his marriage with two other children, his position on the police force that blew up, no wonder Audrey had given him some stipulations to their getting back together. Who knows how much, if any, she knew about his shenanigans. He must have been a charming liar since he told her a bogus reason for leaving the Portland police department.

I found both Dennis and Tana on Facebook in the weeks to follow. I sent them both a friend request and a message to introduce myself. One day, I was working on my computer when I noticed Dennis accepted my request. We started messaging back and forth. He was a bit aloof and didn't know much about his biological father. He told me he didn't even know about him until he was married with kids. All he knew was that his birth father was a police officer in Portland, and his name was Jacques.

The next day Tana accepted my invitation, and we started a long conversation about what I knew about her birth father. I could tell from the tone of her messages she was bitter toward her niece Tiffany and her birth father. Of course, I never knew what all that was about, but it wasn't my business anyway.

I reached out to Dennis again a couple years later; we spoke by text for a while, and I feel like I know him better, but we probably won't be close. In my travels, I will reach out again the next time we get to his state, but I won't hold my breath for more than a meal together.

Unfortunately, at least right now, many of these relationships aren't moving forward. I understand that I bring up emotions in others that may be painful and buried very deep, and when they surface, they can be overwhelming. I'll give it another try after a little more time has passed.

The Honeymoon was Over

My brother Mike, a complicated guy, seemed to get especially close with Loni and her husband, David. I was even a bit jealous because they got along so well. Their sense of humor was similar, and I didn't always get their jokes. I felt like a third wheel at times. Mike moved his trailer onto Loni and her husband's property, and their relationship grew even closer, but their joint negativity affected our relationship. Some things made me uncomfortable, so I started analyzing our friendship. After I looked at it more carefully, I realized I was making most of the effort with Mike and Loni. So I decided to not call them for a while and see what happened. That decision culminated in a couple year break.

Luckily, I was able to rekindle my relationship with Mike when my birth mom fell and sent her to the hospital. My sister Vicki must have called him, and to my surprise, he was at the hospital when I arrived in Bend. We spent several days together while my mom was moved from the hospital to a rehab center, and it was like there had been no time between us. After several long talks, Mike and I got honest about what had happened and why he hadn't continued our relationship. I figured Loni was part of it, but it was easy for him to maintain the distance as he tended to push people away before he was pushed away. I understood, but it hurt just the same. He felt vulnerable, and when things were too good, it was easier to walk out on his own terms rather than be hurt by me or others when we walked away.

Italy with Mike

Luckily my relationship with Mike was renewed after our time in Bend. We started spending more time together again. He came over often, and we began to plan a trip together. In fact, in 2019, we took two extended trips together. Mike & I spent three weeks exploring Italy in May. He had been to Europe while serving in the Vietnam War but hadn't returned. I had taken two trips to Italy previously and loved the area and was excited to go back again. When we started to plan this trip, I was pushing for Italy, but we started planning a trip to England. We started down that path, and then I asked Mike, "If this was the only trip you take back to Europe, is England the place you want to go?" He looked at me and said, "If I only take one trip, I'd prefer to go to Italy." That changed our planning. I was thrilled to share a trip to Italy with my brother. I'd experienced a couple bus tours, so I thought that might be a great way to see Sicily. But I also knew Mike loved to drive; he'd retired after 30 years as a TriMet bus driver, so that element needed to be considered. We decided on the bus tour through Sicily, then rented a car in Rome so he could

Being Silly in Sicily

drive the second half of the trip. We loved driving through the Italian countryside.

Having the freedom to experience little villages and stop for a snack at a sidewalk café was incredible. We went to places we never would have on a bus tour but enjoyed them both. We drove through the Florence countryside, the coastal area of Cinque Terre, and then explored Assisi and surrounding villages, spending three nights in each area.

Mike and I on the Italian Riviera

Mike Showing the View from Wine Tasting

We enjoyed wine tasting at a natural winery, we got lost walking home from dinner one night, and Mike high-centered our rental car on the road near Assisi. The time we spent together was priceless; I'll cherish it always. It was Mike's only trip to Europe, so it made it even more special.

That same year, Vern and I also spent almost three weeks touring many of the National Parks with Mike. We hit locations from Banff, Canada, to the Grand Tetons, Zion, and Bryce Canyon National Parks. Since I journal my trips with photos, I've added a few here to enjoy.

Lake Louise with Mike and Vern

The Rocky Mountains with Mike and Vern

Mike & Vern in Western Bar, Jackson Hole

Wallace, Idaho, with Mike and Vern

Silver Mine Tour

Sabrina, Yet Another Sibling to Meet

So, in September of 2018, I got a message from Tiffany, my niece found through Ancestry, and she said that we had another match. I went to Ancestry, and sure enough, there was another new person. I don't share as many centimorgans with her as I do with my other half-siblings, so I wasn't convinced she was truly a sibling, maybe a first cousin. But if that was the case, my birth father would have a sibling, and he was raised as an only child. Of course, if his father was anything like Jacques, there may be a few sibs we don't know about.

Crazy how all this works sometimes. DNA brings out the best and the worst at times.

Sabrina is a bit younger than me, and after some research, it appears she was another of my half-siblings from my father's side. I was contacted by Art, who wasn't related to me, but to Sabrina. He was fascinated with genealogy and was helping his sister put pieces together of her past. Art and Sabrina share a mom, and she and I share a father. Before it was confirmed, I found some newspaper clippings from the '50s. One article named their mom in an altercation; she had called the police after an older man she lived with became physically abusive. Again, this happened in Portland, OR. Sabrina's mom was a burlesque dancer who worked the San Francisco, Portland and Seattle circuit.

Nine months after the altercation, Sabrina was born. Art & I talked about the stories in the newspaper, and the timing was spot on, so we made the leap that Jacques O'Keefe was also her birth father. I reached out to Sabrina, and we communicated briefly. I spoke to Art more often and realized while I was in California, he and his wife lived less than an hour away from where I was staying. So I reached out to Art and went for a visit in April. We spent about six hours together, and it was great to meet him and his wife and feel so welcomed. We went to dinner, and while Art drove, I was in the back seat behind his wife. Susan, Art's wife, stopped talking for a minute and started to laugh. She said, "If I didn't know any better, I'd swear Sabrina was in the back seat." I guess my voice and my laugh are very much like hers. I found that very exciting, and made me want to meet her even more. I hoped to get to New Mexico in our travels in 2021, and we made the meeting happen. I sent a text to Sabrina about meeting her brother Art and how we were going to be in New Mexico in May. She had talked to Art and got the skinny on me as well. She found out from her brother that I wasn't scary or threatening, so she was more interested in meeting when we were in New Mexico. I was thrilled. I know it can be scary and intimidating, but I was thankful for her willingness.

I know my intentions, but the people I contact have no idea who I am and what I want. Luckily my sincerity comes across quickly, so

I'm thankful for that. Sabrina joined my husband and me for breakfast when we got to her New Mexico area; she also brought her daughter. I was ecstatic to meet yet another niece. The breakfast lasted until lunch, and before we went our separate ways, we decided to have them over the following day for a BBQ. We arranged for them to come by our campground around 3pm. After several hours, I felt pretty good about the start of our relationship. Of all my siblings so far, she and I have the most similarities in looks, voice, and laugh.

Breakfast with Sabrina and Her Daughter

BBQ with Sabrina, Frank, and Apalonia

Stepsister Jennifer

One of the people that has come into my life is
a half-sister to my half-brothers. I know this
gets confusing, so let me explain. After I
reached out to Jacques' boys from his first
marriage, one effort after another got me to a
gal named Jennifer. She is the daughter of the
boy's mother, Neïve, and her second husband,
Henry. She grew up with the boys, and I was
able to ascertain some information about them
from her that I might not be able to receive any
other way. Unfortunately, the youngest of the

two, Patrick, committed suicide in 2016. The oldest brother Michael was his brother's best friend, and Michael was devastated when Patrick took his life. I'm sure the entire family was shocked by such an action, but Michael felt guilty, like he should have known, should have helped. Unfortunately, that's how suicide works. It's a very selfish way to go, leaving a wake of hurt, confusion, and guilt behind. Michael was very hurt, and the pain was unbearable.

For years, he and his brother had heard what a deadbeat dad Jacques was. They heard he didn't help support them or even some of his escapades. Instead, they blamed him for his mother's misery and divorce. His bad feeling about his birth father has affected my ability to get to know Michael firsthand. One silver lining, Jennifer is willing to meet with me and maybe even have a relationship with me. We have talked on the phone, are friends on Facebook, and hopefully will connect again soon. I hope to meet Michael someday, perhaps after he retires. He's a traveling salesman and is gone a lot during the week.

Losing Mike

Mike always felt abandoned by our mom.
When he was three years old, Diane left him
with his father while she took care of her
pregnancy. His dad, Diane's first husband, was
a bit of a bum; he never worked during their
five years of marriage. From Mike's
recollection, he stayed with his dad, but when
his dad married Eddie, his third wife, she forced
Hank to decide, her or Mike. Mike lost that
battle, so at 12 years old, his dad set him up in
an apartment by himself. I have difficulty
believing that any father would do that, but
that's been the story. Abandoned again.

Mike had been married for 25 years; it ended in
divorce, but after both sides of the story came
out, he abandoned his marriage for another
woman. He has been single almost as long as he
was married, but when he talked about his ex,
you would have thought his divorce was recent.
He had a couple daughters, both married now
with their own children. The dissolution of his
marriage took a toll on his relationship with his
kids. Instead of facing their wrath, he
abandoned them before he was abandoned.

Unfortunately, after our trips together in 2019, Mike became more of a hermit. He stayed with Loni and her husband, but he became very antisocial. Covid was tough on his mental health. He tried some travel alone but was depressed and unhappy that he didn't have anyone to share his adventures with. His physical health deteriorated along with his mental health, and when he returned from his travels, he was a shell of the man that went to Italy with me.

Mike has always been difficult; rarely would he make a definitive decision. It was like he couldn't commit, I'm sure it was out of fear, but I never understood him completely.

When Loni's son and daughter-in-law decided to move to North Carolina, he offered to drive their car. He loved the weather, so he stayed, and in early 2022 he was diagnosed with testicular cancer. He started treatment but had some complications with the side effects. The Dr wanted him to do a bronchial test to find out what kind of infection he had in his lungs. Between his lack of ability to make decisions and his short-term memory loss, he didn't give permission for the test, and the infection took his life a few days later. My husband & I were on a trip across the southern states in our RV. Our destination was North Carolina to see him. Unfortunately, we got there too late. He died the morning of the day we arrived. I felt terrible, but we talked on the phone until the last few days. At least we were there to help my niece and nephew go through the things he left behind.

As I remember some of our special memories, I can't forget that I had a relationship with my birth mom and my other siblings because of him. However, it may not have happened had he not pushed Diane to open the communication with me. I believe it was a God thing, and the timing was perfect for the door to open. Luckily with that nudge from Mike, I had a 12-year relationship with Diane and 14 years with him.

Family Dynamics

I want to talk about family dynamics a little more at this point. Everyone's search will be different, and things will be out of your control.

There will be family jokes you won't understand and dysfunctional members of your birth family with whom you won't want to pursue a relationship. Some family members are excited to meet; others give you the cold shoulder and won't talk to you. I have found this interesting, understandable, and disconcerting all simultaneously.

Throughout the ups and downs of adding new people to your family tree, it's important to remember it's not about us. Each person has their own emotions to process. Many unresolved feelings will surface. Some family members may see you as a threat, or they may assume you want to replace them, or some other made-up story they tell themselves. Be yourself, and understand that some people will love you and others won't. Don't take it personally. If they knew you, they would love you, right?

When you open these doors, there will be a honeymoon period where most people will be on their best behavior. But, this good behavior bubble will burst eventually. I found this repeatedly with some of my new connections, some who warmed up immediately, then cooled off just as quickly. Some aren't in my life any longer. Some will return, some won't. Some will be in my life forever. Each relationship is different. It's necessary to be vulnerable and understand that each relationship will have ups and downs. It's essential to grieve all the unmet expectations in those relationships as you go along. Enjoy what is, not what could be. When you have unrealistic expectations, you will be disappointed. To live happily ever after is for fairy tales, not real life. Don't get me wrong, I go into all my new relationships as positively and authentically as possible, with my eyes wide open, with optimism for the future. But I also know I can't expect others to look at life the same way I do.

Timing Can Change Everything

Just because I'm ready for these relationships, not everyone else will be. Remember, no means no, but maybe it means not now. Sometimes opening these doors is a shock. Some people need time to process; many have told themselves a story for years. It may take time to grasp it, different from what they have believed for years. It may open some very touchy, hurtful feelings. I'm dealing with that with my half-brother Michael. He and his brother Patrick were infants when their birth father, Jacques, left them or their mom kicked him out for bad behavior. They never knew him. All they had was what their mom told them. I doubt she had anything good to say about their father. When I reached out to get to know him, Michael couldn't bear to open that floodgate of challenging emotions. The memories of his childhood were painful. His memories of his father were filled with bitterness and feelings of abandonment, etc. So, after all these years, if Michael were to open that door to me, he must open himself up to the pain of his dad not being in his life. Some people aren't equipped to deal with those feelings. I hope he will think about it and, with some encouragement from loved ones, will eventually be able to talk, maybe even meet me. This is a disappointment, but it is my reality. I will try again to reach out and see what happens.

These are perfect examples of me having certain expectations that aren't shared by others. I'd love to know his story and know it from his mother's perspective, but I need to honor his decision even if it isn't my desire. I have texted him a few times with minimal contact. I even called once, and he absently answered his phone, and we had a brief conversation. When he realized it was me, he became vague and unresponsive. He may have blocked me for all I know; I haven't tried since. I will continue to reach out here and there, hoping time will heal at least enough to open the door to meet someday. I hope he doesn't wait too long. As we age, our future isn't certain, as proved by the death of my half-brother Tim, Mike, and Michael's full brother Patrick.

Busting the Dream

You may find some doors slammed in your face when you try to open these doors. That's never the result or reaction we're looking for, but some people can't relive the past. To open a door, even a sliver can expose the past like a million-candlepower light in a dark room. Opening that door can be challenging for all parties concerned. There is always the fear that adoptees may want something from their birth parents. This goes for the siblings as well. People can be wary of the reasons you want to get into their lives.

When I discovered the truth about my mom, that information completely broke apart my fantasy about her. She probably wasn't a great mom; she knew about her daughters' abuse and chose to stand by her man. If I had allowed my judgment or the opinions of others to rule, it would have affected my ability to get to know her. I wouldn't have had a relationship with her. But it was a different time, and I believe it's not my place to judge, even though we all do. I believe she made some horrible decisions, but she paid the ultimate price for those decisions. She didn't have a relationship with most of her kids or grandchildren. And the one she had with her daughter Vicki was only a card or phone call on holidays and an occasional short visit when she was in the hospital. Her relationship with Mike was short-lived when his relationship with Loni revealed the abuse. I'm sure Diane had tremendous guilt over her missteps, but she never discussed those things with me. I tried to help her mend a few of those bridges, but it wasn't to be. They weren't my wounds to heal.

I advise you to be open to the new stories that unfold but not allow them to taint the new ones you create with your new relatives. Don't dwell on the past. The past is important to know about, but it doesn't have to color the future. Getting caught up in the drama is easy, but it's not your drama to fix or live. Instead, create the relationship you want with these new characters in your story. Use your curiosity to delve into the past and put the pieces together.

I believe when I got my Non-ID information from the state in 1996, it shut the door on me because Diane would NOT have opened the door at that point. Her second husband was still alive, and she had not told him about having another baby. She was his caregiver for several years when his health declined. I know in my heart she wouldn't have opened the door back then. In 2008 when I hired Darlene to find her, she was a widow, she had moved to Bend and was being supported emotionally by her sister, so she had the capacity to open the door to me. Timing is important.

What Does the Future Hold?

I hear commercials advertising DNA kits on all platforms, like Ancestry and 23andMe. With all the sales, I expect many thousands, maybe millions more people, to be added to the databases; thus, more potential relatives will be on my dashboard. Each time I open my Ancestry account, I brace myself for a new person to be added to my close family category. I look at the others, but there are thousands. There aren't enough hours in the day to investigate all these people. But close family, first and second cousins, are the ones I can own, try to connect with, and eventually share my story. Once the door is opened, it can't be closed again. Not that I want to close this amazing door which has been an enormous gift to me, but the uncertainty of the knowledge yet to come is always a bit scary. How many more half-siblings will appear, how many will want to connect, and how many will I be able to add value to their lives? Funny, the more answers I find, the more questions I have. I shared my story with a young woman I met at the last retreat I facilitated. She hung on to every word. She was amazed at my story and each new addition I mentioned throughout this journey. She said, "I hope you are writing this all down." I agree with how important all this is. I need to own it and process all the emotions it brings up in me. Plus, that allowed me to revisit my notes when I decided a book would be a great way to share my experiences.

No matter what you find as you set off on your journey, whether it confirms what you think you know about your ancestors or completely blows them out of the water, understand there is always a reason for what you find. As an adoptee, I try to understand the times and circumstances and unravel the stories to find the truth. Although, especially with the advent of DNA results, this may bring conflicting stories to the forefront, it's crucial to understanding the context of the times. I would suggest studying the history and the culture so it's easier to imagine and walk in their shoes before making judgments. Feelings may surface from some of the discoveries, but the truth needs to come out eventually, and now that we have a tool like DNA, it should be an exciting ride. It may cause pain and discomfort for some; however, compassion and understanding of the culture, the times, and circumstances are essential. It's helpful to get the whole picture. Don't allow one unexpected discovery that doesn't match your story to derail your efforts.

The decision to search for my birth parents has changed the course of my life, and it will be yours as well. First, ask yourself if you're ready to hear something other than what you believe. Understanding we may encounter something uncomfortable, embarrassing, or even scary is vital. Taking a DNA test may be the beginning of the roller coaster; make sure you are ready for the ups and downs.

The 50's and 60's were such an interesting time. So many young people were having sex with their partners, and 90% were pregnant within the first year of being sexually active. The funny thing was if the girl got pregnant, she was immediately labeled as the bad girl. If she was lucky not to get pregnant, she was a good girl despite being intimate with her guy. Because of the lack of sexual education and contraception, it was a crapshoot who got pregnant. Even in the 60s, when contraceptives were available, it was illegal for a single woman to get them in many states. The Comstock Law made it illegal to get contraceptives; they were considered "crimes against chastity." So the boys got off scot-free, even when the woman in his life got pregnant. Crazy that there was no judgment for the guys, none. Boys will be boys. Not.

Why is No One Close?

The reason relationships aren't close is because there is too much pain. Trust is broken, and opening yourself up for more is too painful. Opening the door might be ok for curiosity's sake, but a prolonged relationship reminds folks of what they missed or those painful times of loss or cruelty. We can step out of our comfort zone, but having the new becomes the norm means more pleasure than pain. Sometimes the pain wins. I have hoped for extended, close relationships with all I connect with, but that's an unrealistic expectation that will only hurt and frustrate me. We don't have a choice with family, but as an adult without the past to bind us, we choose friends; we don't all mesh. Just because we share blood doesn't mean we will be close.

Vicki is married and had a son and daughter, both with their own children. So she's very close to her family. But none of the siblings are close. The only exception is Diane and Dolores. Dolores lost her husband in 2004, so after Diane's husband died in 2005, Diane decided to move to Bend to be closer to her younger sister. They were best friends.

Dolores and Diane

They spoke twice a day, morning and evening, and saw each other several times a week, whether to go to the grocery store or the casino. I'm so glad they had each other for over a decade to enjoy life without the burden of their husbands.

It was a terrible blow when Dolores passed away before Diane. Since Dolores was younger and had no life-threatening issues, Diane had always expected to go before her sister. Diane had her sister in her will and bank accounts, so she trusted her explicitly. So when she passed suddenly from a fall, Diane was devastated. But the reality that she passed before Diane changed the dynamics of our relationship. She became more open with me and trusted me to do the right thing for her when she passed. We went to the bank, closed her deposit box, and changed Dolores's name to mine on all the important paperwork. She confided in me her burial plans and where she kept all the legal papers I might need. I had earned her trust to be in her inner circle where no one else was.

I have spent a lot of time thinking about how my birth mom has changed my life. I'm thankful for the time I had with her and am grateful for her trust and the emotions she could share with me. I wish I could have had more time with her before her memory got so bad, perhaps I would have some insights I don't have, but I cherished our time together. Because of her, I have four siblings from her. In addition, because of her DNA, I found my biological father and many more half-siblings and have a fascinating story I can share with others searching for their birth families.

The emotions have been all over the map throughout the search and beyond, but they are worth all the ups and downs. It's hard to articulate the feelings around knowing that someone shares your blood. So it was priceless to notice a silly habit or characteristic I shared with my mom. It explains the unexplainable. I'm not the most organized person, but when I opened my mom's closet and found the same piles I make in my home, it gave me a giggle and a nod of understanding. I laughed out loud when I entered her bathroom and found Ponds Cold Cream sitting on her counter. I have used Ponds Cold Cream since I was 14 years old. My mom was thrifty and loved a bargain. I loved to take her shopping and watched her thought process as she found the best price. I tend to be that way as well. Some things are just in you.

Sometimes you can change these things, but many are our default for a reason.

Diane at 90

I remember things about Diane that warmed my heart, like she always got up and dressed immediately. Even before her coffee, she would wear her colorful clothes with matching socks, matching earrings, and necklaces to start the day. She washed her face and combed her hair before leaving the bedroom/bathroom for the morning. You knew she was not feeling well at all if she didn't. Around me, she was generally upbeat, but you could tell she was ornery right underneath the surface.

She was set in her ways but willing to try something new for me, but then would return to her comfortable ways of doing things. She loved to make things to give away, and she supplied baby hats for the hospital most of the years I knew her. She would take over bags of knitted hats to keep babies warm in the hospital and after they went home.

She made blankets, hats and scarf sets, and other crafty items she sold for the cost of her yarn or simply gave away as gifts. She participated in the annual craft bazaar at her apartment complex, keeping her busy all year long preparing and creating new items to display. She finally sold her car when she was 85; she hated to give it up but decided it was best. It symbolized independence to her, and I get that. I can't imagine giving up my car. But she still got out in her scooter; nothing stopped her from buzzing down the street to the Safeway, the bank, Big Lots, the Dollar Tree, and fast-food restaurants.

Epilogue

Diane Justine Kanavel
3/13/1930-11/21/2020

Unfortunately, Diane Justine Hannaford Stockwell Kanavel passed away Nov 21, 2020. She had been in hospice care for almost a year and a half. She didn't die from anything that placed her in hospice care. Her death was because of a terrible fall where she broke her leg in three places. She had talked about death many times with me, and I knew she didn't want to be a burden to anyone, but more than that, she never wanted to be bedridden. She had a couple other falls, one where she fractured her pelvis driving her scooter off a curb backward. We even talked about assisted suicide, so I understood her wishes clearly. I had spent a week with her just eight days before she passed, so even though I was out of town and couldn't get to her fast enough to say goodbye, I knew the end was near. After her fall, the doctor visited her in the hospice house and told her she would never walk again. That night, I got the call. She had passed just after midnight. I planned on driving to Bend that next morning.

But unfortunately, we were there to break the news to her friends at her apartment, make her final arrangements for her cremation and burial, and clean out her place. I was very thankful to my daughter for being willing to make the trip and help. Going through her things was tough. I had tried for the last couple of years to go through a drawer or a closet here and there with her to reduce the sheer number of things she had, but it was a very slow and emotional process for her. It's hard to fathom how a person's life can be summed up this way. I guess that's why I'm not too fond of estate sales for that exact reason. Diane lived in a low-income apartment building, so when we decided to give away almost everything, we had a lot of takers, and it felt great to pass on her things to people who appreciated them and cared about her. We lined the hallways with her stuff as we went through it all, and slowly but surely, most of it disappeared. Most of her things were dispersed to her friends and others in need. My stepdaughter and son also made the trip to show their support and were able to take a couple loads to Goodwill to get rid of the last things before they left to go home.

While we went through Diane's possessions, we found the letters I had heard about in her safe. One was from Cari to her grandmother Kate telling her of the abuse and asking her grandmother to help them get her away from her husband, Fred. What struck me hard from the letter was the inference that Fred beat Diane. The abuse must have been intense to have one of the girls write a letter to her grandma to escape her husband. Diane illuded to me that her life with Fred wasn't great, but she never told me about the abuse she endured. The other letter was from Vicki to her mom, begging her to leave Fred, but neither letter compelled her to leave her husband. My heart hurts that she felt compelled to stay and even care for this man who abused her and his girls. She rests beside her husband Fred in the Willamette National Cemetery on Mt Scott in Portland.

I've thought about my mom's story a lot, wondering specifically why women stay with their abusive husbands and, worse yet, side with them when there is concern about sexual abuse with their children. It's a lot more complicated than I had initially thought. I'm not condoning his behavior, but I understand how it can happen, especially to a woman with low self-esteem, poor education, and few life skills. Diane's father was drunk and abusive to her and her siblings, probably her mom. When she was 17, he threw her out and had all her belongings on the front porch when she came home one evening because he disapproved of the boy she was dating. Unfortunately, this forced her back into the arms of her boyfriend rather than being a deterrent from him. She ended up married with two kids to this man who didn't hold a job their entire marriage. Life was never easy for her, and she was no stranger to abuse.

I think of my mom often, and I'll always be thankful I was able to have a relationship with her. She wasn't a warm cuddly woman, but I have fond memories of us sitting together holding hands, watching a Hallmark movie, or working on a craft project together. She hadn't only opened the door to me and opened her heart as much as she could. I grew to love her for who she was to me, not just the woman who gave birth to me or the mom her children didn't respect, but for the relationship she and I forged over 12 years. Diane, you will be missed. I love you, and it was my pleasure to be your long-lost daughter that found you.

Michael Sandy Stockwell
4/27/1950-5/18/2022

After the trips in 2019, the one in July to many national parks with my husband and the one to Italy, just he and I, we were close again. Then the Covid pandemic hit, and Mike became super depressed. He lived in a fifth wheel on Loni and David's property but became more aloof. The family decided it was time he go since he wasn't participating with the family and was being a hermit. He traveled solo but wasn't taking good care of himself and came home broke and despondent. Later that summer, after regaining his strength, his nephew and his family decided to move back to North Carolina; he offered to help drive a car to the east coast. He stayed in North Carolina for the next 10 months because of the weather. While there, he was diagnosed with testicular cancer. He started treatment, and it was so harsh that he developed mouth sores so severe he couldn't eat or drink. He was dehydrated and malnourished when he entered the hospital in May, developed an infection, and died several days later. My half-brother passed away on May 18, 2022. He was the sibling I've been the closest to since we met in 2008. As we continue our RV travels, I often think, "Mike would love this," or "I should call Mike and tell him about this," etc. I miss him dearly; he had a rough exterior with a negative attitude, but he was a sweet, scared little boy I loved very much.

Tip for Your Search

Adoptions are either open or closed. Open adoptions have become more prevalent in the last few decades. Open adoption allows all parties to know each other, keep in contact, share photos, have conversations, and be friends or family. Closed adoptions are just that, closed. The adoption papers are sealed by a judge to keep the transaction private with the thought they wouldn't ever be opened.

Every state has different laws surrounding the release of closed adoption records. Each state also has procedures to obtain records from a closed adoption. All states have documentation to obtain the original birth certificates, some more difficult than others. Usually, it's the bureau of records or vital records departments you'll need to contact to obtain an original birth certificate if it has been sealed. This is the same department you would contact to get a marriage license.

To obtain your original birth certificate, you must be at least 18 years old and the child or one of the parents listed on the certificate. The adoptive parents are not allowed to access these records.

Some states, like Oregon, will release the birth certificate automatically if you fill out the forms and follow the correct procedures. However, some states may complicate this process and deny your request. Therefore, you may have to contact your state representative to get their help to release the information. A call or email to their office can help expedite the process or get a denial overturned.

Either way, a judge will need to sign off on your request. The process for arranging that appointment is by filing a petition. The petition is a relatively simple form that needs to be filed with the county court. When filling out the form, you have a better chance if your reasoning isn't based solely on personal desire or interest. For example, medical issues are the most common reason sealed adoption records are unsealed.

The judge will either grant your petition and unseal the records or deny your petition. If this happens, you can request a confidential intermediary or, as I did, hire an intermediary from the start.

If you were adopted through an agency or unwed mother home, you might be able to get information from the agency that placed you. Often the agency or lawyer used for the adoption also has information filed away, so it's worth some time and energy to find out what they have and if you can access that information. Generally, they will try to contact the individuals whose information you are looking for and gain their consent to release the information.

There are organizations in most states to help support an adoptee in finding their birth families. In addition, I have seen people in social media groups on Facebook who are very knowledgeable and willing to help with suggestions on how best to search. Those willing to help are called angels for apparent reasons. If I were to do this research today, I would ask people in these groups as many questions as possible to get some advice and search direction.

Don't forget to ask your state for your Non-ID information. There may be a small cost for it, but it will give you some information that might be helpful in your search. Please don't believe everything it says until you see your genuine birth certificate. Remember my mom's fictitious name? But it will get you started. If you were born in another country other than the United States, your search would be different, but there may be similarities to remember.

There are also numerous online adoption reunion registries where birth parents and adoptees searching for information can register. Sometimes, a match can be made if both are searching and have registered.

If you have even the slightest bit of information, like a name and approximate age, you might be able to find the person you are looking for with a quick Google search or a search on Facebook. It might help narrow your search like I did for my birth father's widow. But, as I mentioned earlier, searching on social media can also open doors. Here are a few reunion registries; some are free, some are not, so do your own research, but this will get you started.

https://adoption.org
https://adoption.com
https://www.reunionregistry.org
https://registry.adoption.com
International Soundex Reunion Registry
https://adoptionnetwork.com

DNA Testing Kits

There are many DNA tests available; I did three different tests myself. I have found that ancestry.com and 23andme.com are the most used, which means they have extensive databases which open you up to the most potential matches. I have found that younger people tend to use 23andme.com, and older people use ancestry.com a bit more often. That's why I found it helpful to do both. On 23andme, I found a couple of nieces and nephews that led me to half-siblings, and they hadn't done ancestry.

DNA raw data analysis files hold more than is typically provided by sites like Ancestry or 23andMe. In addition, there are numerous platforms where you can upload your raw information to learn even more. I went through this process but haven't followed up on any results since I've focused on contacting my matches.

When I refer to matches, if you do one of the DNA kits and one of your birth relatives has also done a kit on the same platform, they will pop up in your results as a relative. It might not be the person you are looking for, but they might have information that could be useful to you. I have found that most people who do a DNA kit are willing to talk about it; they are curious about things like you are. I generally message them through the platform and hope I get a response. If they don't respond in a couple of days, I try to look them up on Facebook, LinkedIn, Instagram, etc., to see if I can find them and message them through those platforms.

Centimorgans Chart

cM (centiMorgans)^		Percentage (%) of Shared DNA^^		Group	Relationship	Notes
Average	Range	Average	Range			
3,800		50%			Parent - Child	
2650	2300 - 3900	37%	32%-54%	Group A	Full Sibling	Ancestry, FTDNA and GEDmatch (HIR only)
3600		66%				23andMe (FIR included)
1800	1300 – 2300	25%	18%-32%	Group B	Half Sibling Aunt/Uncle/Niece/Nephew Double First Cousin Grandparent/Grandchild	3/4 Siblings^^^
900	575 - 1330	12.5%	8%-18.5%	Group C	First Cousin (1C) Half Aunt/Uncle/Niece/Nephew Great-Grandparent/Great-Grandchild Great-Aunt/Uncle/Niece/Nephew	
450	215 - 650	6.25%	3%-9%	Group D	First Cousin Once Removed (1C1R) Half First Cousin (½ 1C) Half Great-Aunt/Uncle/Niece/Nephew	
224	75 - 360	3.125%	1%-5%	Group E	Second Cousin (2C) First Cousin Twice Removed (1C2R) Half First Cousin Once Removed (½1C1R)	
112	30 - 215	1.96%	0.42% - 3%	Group F	Second Cousin Once Removed (2C1R) Half Second Cousin (½ 2C) First Cousin Three Times Removed (1C3R) Half First Cousin Twice Removed (½ 1C2R)	
56	0 - 109*	0.78%	0% - 1.52%	Group G	Third Cousin (3C) Second Cousin Twice Removed (2C2R)	~10% of 3Cs will not share DNA*
30	0 - 75**	0.4%	0%-1%	Group H	Third Cousin Once Removed (3C1R) Other Distant Cousins	~50% of 4Cs will not share DNA**

DNA Detectives Autosomal Statistics Chart
Created by Christa Stalcup · ©THEDNADETECTIVES, 2016

^cM =Ancestry.com & FTDNA
^^Percentage of DNA = 23AndMe
^^^ 3/4 Siblings are a combination of half siblings and 1st cousins, FIRs are included.

Groups A & B: 99% within the ranges given
Groups C – I: 95% within the ranges given

I'm not a genealogy expert, but this chart was helpful when I started getting matches from my DNA. For instance, my half-brother Tim & I share 1,772 cM (centimorgans), which is 25% shared DNA. His daughter and I share 1,101 cM, and 16% shared DNA which shows she's my half-niece. The science behind DNA is very complicated and way over my head, but this will give you a place to start, and as you go through your journey, ask questions of people who have studied this science in more depth.

There will be starts and stops but be persistent. Some people go as far as to hire private investigators because their need to connect is so great. Even if you must knock on more than a few doors to get the information you seek, finding your birth family is worth it. Don't procrastinate. We are all getting older, and there's no better time to start your journey than right now.

Timing is everything too. You may need to put your search on the back burner when you hit a brick wall, but pull it back out and keep looking. Technology is changing, laws change, and feeling change, so what feels like a brick wall today might be little or no problem tomorrow.

https://ancestry.com
https://www.23andme.com
https://www.myheritage.com
https://www.familytree.com

Adoption reunions can be challenging for many reasons, but the loss and pain of the separation of birth parent and child seem to top the list. Some feelings bubble up that may surprise you, and some might be feelings of mistrust and fear even before the search begins. This may be a bumpy road, but it's worth it. You will grow in the process, and with growth comes some pain. I wish you the best of luck in your search.

I've included a family tree for my birth mother and father to clarify who is who.

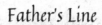

Father's Line

Michael
5/6/1954

Tana
4/14/1957

Patrick
9/26/1953

Tim
4/21/1952

Sharon
9/17/1953

Sabrina
8/21/1955

Dennis
2/13/1956

Nieves

Virginia

Diane

Wilma

Elayne

Jacques

DNA

D... Do

N... Not

A... Assume

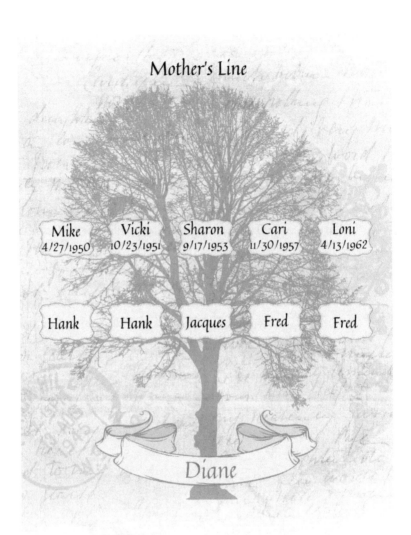

Mike	Vicki	Sharon	Cari	Loni
4/27/1950	10/23/1951	9/17/1953	11/30/1957	4/13/1962

Hank	Hank	Jacques	Fred	Fred

Diane

Made in United States
Troutdale, OR
07/03/2023